Bo
Yriri.

BEHIND
the
BUTT⊙N

You will inspire
The world.
So happy to be on
this Journey with
You

BEHIND
the
BUTT●N

My Journey in Life and Fashion
and How They Are Interwoven

JILL STRICKLAND BROWN

Bright
COMMUNICATIONS

Printed in the United States of America
Published in Hellertown, PA

Cover and interior design by Joanna Williams

Library of Congress Control Number: 2021905277
ISBN 978-1-952481-12-3

2 4 6 8 10 9 7 5 3 1 paperback

Bright
COMMUNICATIONS

To all the empowered women

Who have empowered me

CONTENTS

INTRODUCTION

LIFE IS LIKE A DYEBATH. My background is in garment-dyed clothing, and it was the backdrop to my life. There are so many parallels. When clothing is dyed, the garment is immersed in scalding hot water, beaten with paddles, and agitated as the dye seeps into the fabric. Sometimes in life, we feel like we're being thrown into a dyebath—being stressed and tested almost to our limits.

The dyebath is transformative. In addition to changing the color of the garment, it changes the fibers structurally as well. The fibers react to the water and heat. In the end, the garment is stronger and more beautiful than it was before—just like how women emerge more beautiful with lines and stretch marks, badges of honor of a life well lived.

A dyebath creates a unique, one-of-a kind garment. No two pieces of garment-dyed clothing are the same.

The result of a dyebath is a longer-lasting garment. Because a dyebath is hard on fabric, manufacturers must start out with better-quality fabrics—those able to withstand the bath. Then the process itself toughens the fabric. Dyebaths can create a vintage, distressed look—apropos of the struggles the fabrics have endured.

Like most women, I've gone through my fair share of dyebaths in my life. I spent my life struggling to be the daughter, sister, wife, mother, and entrepreneur that everyone wanted me to be.

When I began to overcome the challenges in my life, it was transformative for me. I'm better and stronger because of them. And without them, I would not have this story to tell.

Often, we look in the mirror and see our flaws. We try desperately to hide those flaws from others, only showing others our curated lives on social media. In time, I've grown to embrace my uniqueness, and I appreciate my eccentricities as the "irregularities" of life. I started to believe in me.

I've learned that it's okay to be vulnerable and let others see these parts of me. In fact, it was when I allowed myself to be vulnerable I felt the most connected I've ever been.

Often, when we allow ourselves to be vulnerable, we realize our friends have been struggling, too. They've been right next to us in the dyebath all along. We are all connected; we are all interwoven.

I've learned that choosing quality, well-made garments over cheap, throwaway clothing is like doing the tough work to grow instead of trying to do things the fast, easy way. In the industry, we call them "investment pieces." In my life, it was worth it to do the work, to invest in myself. It was what I needed to do to thrive.

In this book, I share the story of how I wove together the threads of my life into a tapestry I'm proud of. From my decades of time in the fashion industry, I've learned the value of creating your life to suit *you* and in choosing the clothing to suit *your life*—designing the best version of you inside and out.

I know this from helping of thousands of women transform right in front of my eyes as I teach them about fit and drape and how to best accentuate their unique body type.

That feeling of empowerment through personal transformation has a ripple effect on not only how we see ourselves but how we are seen in the world. When you help a woman, everyone benefits: family, friends, and communities. It is the ultimate trickle down.

I realize that I will always be going through dye-baths—ever transforming, ever changing. This book is my story, the story of Frox, my beloved boutique and my love of fashion, and it's your story, too. I hope that you see yourself in these pages and be inspired to share your journey in my next book where I will share the stories of other empowered women. You will notice that threaded through the book you will find fashion tips that I have collected over my 30-year career

It's my mission to help you to become the person you are destined to be—to design your best life—both inside and out. By believing in yourself and with hard work, tenacity, and resilience, you can emerge from life's dyebaths stronger and better.

CHAPTER 1

The Fabric

THE THREAD THAT RUNS THROUGH my life are the women who have influenced me, mentored me, and made me the strong woman I am today, and it all started with my mom.

My mom grew up in Philadelphia. She was stunning, looking much like Jackie Kennedy. In one of my favorite photos of my mother, she had her hair full and flipped up at the ends with a headband, and she wore a black turtleneck, suede bolero vest, stirrup pants, and penny loafers. Of course I remember everything about her outfit, my love of fashion started early. My mom was brought up with traditional values of the time. She went to charm school and

My mom

secretarial school. Back then, the thinking was that a young woman should go to school to bide her time until she was married. Throughout my life, I watched her evolve into the strong empowered woman she is today.

My parents met at a dance at a synagogue in 1956. It was a whirlwind romance; they were married a few months later. After my parents got married, my father wanted to raise their family in New York or Philadelphia to have all the culture that he experienced growing up in New York City on the Hudson River.

My paternal grandmother

His father was an inventor who founded a now-100-year-old conglomerate that is still operating today. His most successful invention was a means of reading from printed film. This process was adopted by the Library of Congress, where one million volumes have been photographed. Instead of taking up acres of space, they are conveniently and permanently recorded on small motion picture reels.

My paternal grandfather

The reels were also sold to book lovers who could enjoy them by means of another one of my grandfather's inventions, the "Easy Reader." The idea was that while you relaxed in your chair or bed, his device enlarged and illuminated each successive film frame, comparable to a page of a book. A slight movement of the hand on the remote control brought successive frames in view. Sound familiar? It was a form of an early e-book that we use today without any thought to its origins. My grandfather secured more than 56 patents in his life. My grandmother lived long after him and shared his successes with her family.

Because of the success of my grandfather, my dad led an opulent life. Although it didn't come without a struggle. His dad died when he was young, and his mom was not domestic. So, he was raised by nannies and sent to military school. As a native New Yorker, he loved all things New York. He experienced the finest culture, food, and films that came from there. My dad was extremely good looking and charismatic. With dark hair graying at the temples and fashionable glasses, he resembled Cary Grant. My mom, of course, was very attracted to him.

Soon after my mother and father visited a utopian community being built outside the city called Levittown, Pennsylvania, my parents bought one of the first Levittown houses. My dad paid $16,000 for the house—cash, from one of his inheritances.

Their home was a medium-sized, Cape Cod–style house. We entered a large living room that led to the

My parents' wedding

kitchen. Behind that were my parents' room and the bathroom. My dad took over the den as his office. Upstairs there was one big bedroom and one little bedroom. My mom and dad raised five kids in that tiny house, which was so different from the mini mansions we see today.

One day when my two oldest sisters were little, everything changed. A knock on the door altered the trajectory of our lives forever.

My mother surely must have been searching for something. As she looked through that door, perhaps it wasn't the utopian life she imagined. The woman at the door must have offered my mother the right message at the right time. The visitor invited my mother to study the Bible. My

My parents' first house in Levittown

mother says it saved her. "It made me happy, and I love the people," she'd say. It was the community that called her. She soon converted to become one of Jehovah's Witnesses, far from the Jewish faith she knew. My dad kept his Jewish faith.

My mother said that if she had not joined the religion, she would have been part of the women's movement. She wanted to be part of something bigger than herself. She passed that longing on to me. My mom has always been extremely smart and loved the education and studying aspect of her new religion as well.

Even though we had a life and a home in Levittown, my dad didn't fit in well there. Levittown couldn't compete with the city—because it simply wasn't New York.

The community of Levittown was built on the richest

My mom, my siblings, and me

soil in Bucks County, Pennsylvania. It was one of the first planned developments in the country, the epitome of small-town America. I could walk or ride my bike everywhere without having to cross or even walk on a big street. Neighbors were friendly, and they watched out for each other. While I enjoyed growing up in a picturesque, small community in Bucks County, I felt I had a little life there. I was always drawn to the drama, excitement, and bustle of the big city just like my dad. Even as a young child I yearned for so much more. Sometimes where you are is not where are meant to be.

One very bright spot from my childhood was our annual trip to Broadway. Each year, my dad drove the whole family to New York to see a play around holiday time for our holiday gift. The purpose was the play, but a huge side benefit for me was to see the holiday windows on Fifth Avenue. Seeing all those windows influenced me as a girl, and it still does to this day. Those store windows inspired my own. I continued this annual NYC-trip tradition many years later with my own children. Those trips were the best gifts my dad could have given us. He gave us

An ad for our Levittown house

an experience instead of plastic toys that were going to be gone in a short time. He gave us memories that will last a lifetime. Just like a zipper, your dreams pull you toward them. Those trips made my New York dreams become closer and closer each year.

My dad was very eccentric. He loved boating, and he had two sailboats—a Lightning and a Laser. My dad enjoyed spending his free time at the yacht club and puttering around in his workshop and den. I always felt he didn't have time for me; he was always caught up in his projects. He did contract work; therefore, sometimes our family had enough money, but other times we had very little. The work was unsteady. Sometimes he would go long periods of time without a job. My mother did not work out of the home as she was caring for five children.

My dad's money went to boating and the yacht club. He no longer wanted to be part of our family. He wanted the life of the yacht club. When my dad wasn't at the yacht club, or at work, he was building things in his shop or alone in his den.

As a child, I didn't understand why he had money for boats but not for us. My dad withheld even the basic necessities of food and clothing from us. He'd send us to our rooms with only bread and water, or he'd banish us to eat out in the dirty garage which was filled with saw

My parents

dust and metal shavings from tools in which he used to fabricate things for the boat. I remember eating meals on a chipped pink metal trunk staring at all the cobwebs in the shop.

My dad never talked about his rough childhood. Back then, I didn't know what challenges he had or how or they affected him.

Recently, I learned that he struggled his whole life to reach the success of my grandfather. That is why he was always in the shop. He was trying to invent the next big thing. Knowing that allows me to understand him now.

One day, my dad was especially furious. He knocked

my mom to the ground. Then he towered over her with one leg on each side of her hips. He made a fist, pulled back his arm, and looked like he was going to hit her. Always the scrappy fighter, at 10 years old, I ran up behind him and jumped on his back screaming, "Stop!" Shocked at my actions, he came out of his state and let her up. My sister told me after this day everything shifted. She said, "The day before things were okay because he only hit us. But after this day, we knew he would hit our mom, too."

At the time, corporal punishment was accepted, and my dad used that in many forms on us—sometimes holding us up by our feet and hitting us with a belt or ruler. If we really were "bad," he would give a pants-down spanking, which was humiliating and degrading.

This affected all of my siblings and me, each in different ways. The grown-up versions of ourselves never spoke of how this truly affected each of us, but we are all left with our own ways of dealing with it. For me, the effects lasted into adulthood. I was unable to be vulnerable and open up. I built a wall around my heart, always fighting to protect myself. This was how I started to develop my tenacity and fighting spirit, which I would need to survive. I never expected to get anything more than the scraps of love I was given. I didn't feel worthy of love and protection. This would be one of the first dyebaths that I would come to endure and certainly not the last!

We got most of our clothing from bags sent home from the congregation. I was even afraid to ask my dad for new shoes. I remember my feet curling up in my shoes at school. I often felt like a burden. I was just there. To be seen, not heard. Be small, hang low, and you won't get hurt. I never knew which dad I was going to get: happy dad who took us to the beach or bring home special pumpernickel bread and gorgonzola cheese from his trips to Philadelphia, or erratic dad, violently yelling, screaming, and hitting us.

The silver lining was since I never knew which dad I was going to get, I learned how to read people really well. I do that to this day in my shop. I can tell when a customer comes in if she is happy, sad, anxious, or nervous. I can tell when she has tried on too many things and is hitting her limit. I took my mess of a childhood and made it my message.

Before each new school year, my mom would take us to a local department store called Two Guys, which was much like a Walmart of today. She would line up all five of us, and we'd each get one new outfit. It was not much, but I remember to this day one of my new outfits was a

One of my favorite outfits

red jacket with contrasting plaid pockets and matching plaid pants. It was oh so '70s. I was happy to have a new outfit for the first day of school. Today, I think that might be why I chose a career in fashion and opened my own clothing store. Now I have all the clothing I could ever need or want.

Growing up, we didn't have much, but we always found a way to survive. I have great memories of my sisters. I remember playing with two of my older sisters a lot. We didn't have a lot of toys, so we used our imaginations. We'd play games, pretend our living room TV was a drive-in movie theater, with Barbie dolls as the audience, have picnics, and play school. Some days I pretended to be the "good student"; other days I pretended to be the "bad student." We didn't have a chalkboard, so we wrote on the back of our bedroom door. I'm sure our parents loved that. Our hallway had a tile floor, and we'd kneel on pillows and pretended they were canoes.

As was common in the seventies, my siblings and I enjoyed a lot of free, unstructured play. We were fortunate to grow up in a safe, small community. We made forts and played outside for hours. My mom would send us out in the morning, saying, "Come back when the streetlight comes on."

"Go outside, knock the stink off," my dad would say.

We went to the neighbors' houses, played kickball, rode our bikes—no helmets back then. When you fell you picked yourself up, wiped off the rocks and blood, and kept going. We would walk down to the creek. When the creek flooded, we swam in it.

As I reflect, back this was such a different time. My children did not have this freedom of unstructured play. Their childhood was very structured with many sports.

I remember being afraid to let them outside because something might happen to them. There was much more indoor play, video games, and TV. I think that in my youth, we were allowed to play life on a small scale so that when big things came up later, we knew how to handle them.

Another childhood tradition I remember fondly is our daily trips to Penn Warner Lake, which is in nearby Tullytown, Pennsylvania. My dad taught us how to sail. We would go to the middle of the lake, and when we got hot, we would capsize the boat and swim. It popped right back up because it was just a cockpit and a sail. My mom brought a hibachi to grill hot dogs and chicken legs right on the picnic table. After supper, I'd lie belly down on the wooden dock and dangle the chicken bones into the water for the sunfish to nibble on. We picked ripe, juicy blackberries, which tasted better than any sweet-tart candy you could imagine.

When it was rainy and we couldn't go to the lake, we would sit in our room and read for hours. I remember reading the Books of Knowledge, the entire Nancy Drew series, all of the Mary Poppins books, and so many more. They took me off to distant places that I would never experience in my small town. Today I use books to inspire me. I am

(continued on page 30)

INVESTMENT PIECE:
THE LITTLE BLACK DRESS

Another outfit I remember fondly: my blue-and-white gingham dress. It was the style of the time. But now I teach my ladies to buy trends sparingly and pair them with classic pieces.

Today, a staple of my wardrobe is a little black dress: LBD.

My LBD is a boatneck shift dress, which is perfect for my body shape. It's a straight dress that skims over my belly and hips. Because I'm petite, it's above the knee. It's classic. I can put it on anytime and feel great. I feel put together.

Your LBD is an investment piece. It's a staple of your wardrobe. If you go to an event or party, it's right in the middle. You won't look underdressed or overdressed. Here's how to buy one:

- Invest in quality. Don't skimp on this purchase. It should last you for years.
- Choose a classic cut, such as an A-line that will stand the test of time. Don't follow a fad.
- Select a classic, face-flattering neckline, such as a scoop or boatneck.
- For four-season wearability, buy a sleeveless silhouette that can be layered with a jacket or wrap.
- Buy a quality fabric, such as linen, rayon, or cotton. For winter, consider a gabardine or wool crepe.

always listening to and quoting motivational books. So many threads of knowledge have been incorporated in my life and in this book. I am still blown away that I am writing my own.

When I was little, on July 4th, we'd lie on the windshield of my parents' station wagon and watch the fireworks. The station wagon had a rear-facing seat in the very back. We called it the "back back," and we fought over who got to sit there.

Things were so different back then. Safety rules were relaxed—for better or worse—and this gave us glimpses of my mom's wacky side. Sometimes, when we'd stop at stoplights, my mom would yell, "Fire Drill!" All of us kids would leap out of the station wagon, run around it, and hop back in before the light turned green.

When we got a little older, my oldest sister and I did crafts. She taught me how to crochet, work with leather, paint, and do calligraphy. We would bead and make friendship bracelets. My sister was very crafty; she still is. Today, she owns a knitting company, and she teaches knitting as well. I remember this being one of my favorite things to do—being with my sister and creating beautiful things.

I have straight hair, and my youger sister had curly hair. Of course, we always wished we had the opposite hair type. My mom usually braided my hair and secured the braids with elastics that had two plastic balls on the ends. Every picture of me is in those braids. When my mom brushed my hair, I would yell because it pulled on the knots.

Me and my braids

"I'm gonna cut your hair into a pixie cut," my mom would joke.

Years later, I *did* get a pixie cut. I remember thinking, *I got the haircut that she always teased me about.* When life gets you in knots, just untangle a little at a time.

Growing up, our faith was a big part of our lives. It created a lot of struggle in school and home.

But I believe that struggle is made to see if you rise— to see what you are made of. We were not allowed to celebrate holidays or the events surrounding them. We didn't pledge allegiance to any man-made government. This meant being sent to the library or principal's office at school when any holiday events happened. I was never allowed to be part of the celebration. When anything patriotic like the "Star-Spangled Banner" was played or the morning Pledge of Allegiance was recited, I had

A convention of my faith Bible instruction at JFK stadium

been taught to not participate and sit. I feared that any disobedience would result in displeasing my God. At the time, there was no tolerance for people of other faiths. But I wanted to be part of things. I wanted to fit in. Teachers created a narrative that I was being rebellious and would scream in my face to comply. Then they'd send me to the principal's office for a reprimand. This taught me at a young age to be resilient, just like fabric's resilience having the ability to return to its original form after being bent or compressed.

At home, I was a high-spirited kid. Everyone called me a little firecracker. When I was 13, I must have pushed my mom to her limit. She screamed at me, "I'm going to break your spirit!"

I stomped up the stairs repeating on each step loudly, "You are never going to break my spirit!" I knew even in my youth I was destined to be so much more. I had the spark to do great things; I just didn't know how I was going to make my mark in the world. This was the start of my can-do spirit.

As I became more self-aware, I realized that the

Me dressed to go into the preaching work

gift I bring to the world is the best version of me. I believe we are all unique and beautiful in our own way—just like the unique garments emerging from a dyebath.

Looking back now I most likely got some of that from my mom. I remember she'd go around the house singing "I Will Survive" by Gloria Gaynor. That was her anthem, her little spark of fire. She also had a rebellious streak. My dad did not like pink and purple, so after he left, she painted his special den purple and her room pink. This was one of the ways she got her power back. My mom also gained strength and confidence from her faith, which included preaching at people's homes.

I was taught at an early age to go door to door and speak in public. From that experience, I learned that I can do anything. If you can overcome that fear of talking to someone on their doorstep about the Bible, you can pretty much do anything you set out to do. I told myself, *This person is busy and may not be interested in what I have to say and probably wants to throw me off their step, but if I find our common ground, I might get my message through.* This experience instilled in me the desire to speak boldly about something bigger than myself, particularly in the service of others. I believe these seedlings blossomed into my desire today to speak and share my message of inspiration and empowerment with as many people as I can.

As a kid, after school, sometimes I was allowed to watch a little TV only after chores and homework were done. We would watch *The Brady Bunch*, and then my dad would come home and say, "Turn off that idiot box. Go read a book." I most likely got my love of books from him.

My dad also had a great vocabulary, and he would use very big words. When we didn't understand him, he would say, "Go look it up," and dispatch us off to the large dictionary on the kitchen table to find out the meaning. No Google back then. That early training has served me well, even though I struggle with a learning disability. I have found many tools to help me. I am addicted to Siri and spell check. I listen to many books instead of reading them. I have learned from many of the great inspirational speakers that there will always be obstacles. But it is how you overcome them that counts. I am most proud of overcoming obstacles—even more than I am proud of my achievements. When I started writing this book, I began to believe in myself. I never imagined writing anything down because my whole life I struggled with writing. But as I wrote each chapter, my confidence grew. I am happy because I now have another way to give to others.

When I was younger and home sick from school, my mom would allow TV. We called it a "Lucy break" because we watched *I Love Lucy*. TV watching back then was more of an event than today's mindless TV watching.

Lucy was cool. I loved her '50s style. My mom was a

(continued on page 38)

BEAUTIFUL
INSIDE AND OUT

USE COLOR TO CHANGE A MOOD

Color has a tremendous impact on our mood. When my mom painted her room pink, it created a mood in that room—happy, girly, fun, rebellious.

The colors you wear will influence your mood, and they will even influence the mood of people around you. And through your choice of color, you can express your own style.

Certain colors evoke particular moods or feelings. For example:

- Red = power
- Orange = safety
- Yellow = happiness, warmth
- Green = nature, health
- Blue = calmness, serenity
- Purple = royalty
- White = purity, cleanliness
- Black = grief, or chic

If you wear the right color for your skin tone and hair coloring, you will notice a glow in your skin, and your eye color will pop. You can find your best colors by using a color wheel. You might have learned about the color wheel in your elementary school art class. This tool is used universally when creating colors. The wheel consists of three colors in a circle, with red and blue on the cool side of the wheel and yellow on the warm side. All colors are derived from these three colors. So, all you need to know is which side of the wheel you are on.

Usually, you can tell by the color on the inside of your wrist. If your skin has blueish hues, you are cool toned. You will look better in red and blues, often soothing colors that remind you of water, sky, and ice, such as brilliant blue and deep purple eggplant. If your wrist has yellowish tones, you are warm toned. Gravitate toward warmer colors that are based in yellow or green. Think warm, sunshine colors such as sunflower yellow and autumn pumpkin.

Think about your favorite color. You likely are drawn to colors that look best on you. If you love pinks, blues, and purples, you are likely a cool tone. If you prefer oranges, yellows, and browns, you're probably a warm tone.

Use this information to choose the best colors for your clothing—and also to choose the best colors for your hair and even your home décor. You will be surprised how great surrounding yourself with your perfect colors will make you feel.

Buttoned Up

ADD VALUE

Success in business—just like success in life—is all about relationships. You build your business one relationship at a time. Little did I know at the time how much those hours spent talking in people's doorways about the Bible would help me be the entrepreneur I am today.

People are busy, and they have nearly limitless options to spend their money. To get them to spend their time with you—at your business—you must add the value that only you can bring.

I'm competing against faceless online retailers, where shopping is impersonal. The customer can look at herself in the mirror and say, "Oh, that's cute." What I offer is a more refined opinion. I can answer their deeper questions: How is this going to drape on my body? How do I care for it? Once I have educated a customer, she wants to come

'50s mom, so she had really cool clothes. Years later, I looked at pictures of her and said, "Mom, I love this! It's totally back! Why didn't you save your clothes for me?"

"Are you saving your clothes for your kids right now?" she asked.

"I guess not," I replied.

Even now, my daughter will come in with her clothes from Urban Outfitters and ask, "What do you think?"

back. When I suggest she try on something that she never thought would work for her and she ends up looking great, I build trust. Also, when you explain the many ways in which a garment can be used, the customer learns that the cost per wear goes down. When people come to Frox to buy clothes, they walk away with an education. I teach them how to choose clothing that accentuates their positives—and downplays their figure flaws. I explain why a particular fabric drapes the way it does and why that makes them look fantastic. And I explain that when you invest in quality clothing, wearing it makes you feel great, and it takes away the stress of wondering how you look. Wearing the right clothing makes you feel confident. You can be authentically yourself because you feel amazing.

I'll say, "I think I wore that 20 years ago!" I love how everything comes full circle: life and clothing.

My childrens clothing has been store bought, but my mom made all of our clothes. My mom used sit at her old black-and-gold Singer sewing machine. I remember her pushing the pedal, and the machine would fly. She'd buy a bolt of fabric and some McCall's patterns and hand make clothing for all of us and even jackets for my dad.

In stores, she'd whisper to me, "I can make it better than that." This inspired me to be creative and resourceful.

I also remember my mom getting ready at her vanity table. It had curtains and drawers and a circle mirror. She fixed her hair in a cool sixties style and applied her signature pink lipstick. I remember just watching and admiring her. Today as I sit at my vanity, I work on loving myself and liking what I see, which is the hardest work of all.

My grandmother was someone I mirrored. We actually called her "Nanny." When we asked her if she wanted to be called Grandma or Granny, she said, "I am too young to be a grandma. Call me Nanny." She brought out the best in us. She knew that we are all born with a purpose; we all have unique gifts. People say I look and act like her—with her short auburn hair and fine, delicate features. Her inner light made her glow with beauty inside and out. My Nanny was an "influencer" long before that word was coined. When she entered a room, she lit it up. People were always excited to see her and to be in her presence. She was funny and stylish. One of my favorite memories of her is when she wore a bell-bottomed pant-suit and white boots, striding into the room like it was a New York runway. Self-confidence oozed from her.

My nanny and mom

I have happy memories of simple fun with Nanny in her 55-plus community. We went bike riding, hung by the pond, and played shuffleboard in the clubhouse. Our secret escape was watching *All My Children* and *General Hospital* on TV. My grandmother would invite her friends over, and

My nanny

she liked to show me off. I would play hostess and serve them drinks on a tray. My visits with her made me feel special and loved.

On Sundays, my grandmother "Nanny" and my grandfather "Hank" would come over. It was the highlight of my week. My siblings and I would race down the street to greet them and run alongside their car until they pulled into our driveway. Nanny would talk and be with us. I felt so special just being around her. They always brought us candy, which was a special treat.

When my grandparents visited, we were allowed to watch *The Wonderful World of Disney*. That was a treat.

After the show, my siblings and I went to bed, and my

Nanny and Hank

parents and grandparents played pinochle. I would listen to them playing from my bed. When I heard them say, "Schnitzel," it indicated the end of the game, and I knew my grandparents would be leaving for the night. Before they were out the door, I'd fall asleep.

Nanny's brothers and sisters lived in the Philadelphia

area. I remember going to their houses in the city. I can still see the plastic covers on their fancy furniture and hard candies in little bowls. They talked of going to Wanamaker's for tea, wearing white gloves and lunch suits. An oil painting of one of my great-grandmothers hung on the wall of their apartment. She was beautiful, wearing a pink suit with gray epaulets. I loved her style. The people from that branch of my family tree seemed very urban and sophisticated to me.

Nanny and I had a unique bond. One thing I learned from her was to be wholly myself. There was something special about her. And she felt the same about me. She once told my mom, "This one is different." This meant so much to me because usually my siblings and I were lumped together as a group. Even though I was one of five children, she always made me feel important—and seen. She loved life—especially celebrating. I am very much like her in this way.

When my grandmother died, she left a huge void in my life and hole in my heart.

Nanny closed the loop. In clothing terms, closing the loop is making sure the fabric is natural and pure, so it is kind to the earth at the end of the cycle. Nanny was the kindest person, and she left this earth better because she was here.

Later, my grandfather moved in with us to help around

At the apartment in the city.

the house. He used to say it was hard on him because I reminded him of her. He would tear up and say, "You look like and remind me of her so much." That was the best compliment he could ever have given me.

CHAPTER 2

The Thread

ONE DAY, WHEN I WAS 13, I went out to the garage, which was my dad's domain. To spend time with my dad, I needed to share his interests. Like my grandfather, my dad was a tinkerer. His garage was messy, packed with welding and metal fabricating equipment.

"What are you doing?" I asked.

"I'm moving my stuff to my office," he replied.

I didn't believe him because I saw he was packing up *all* his stuff.

I knew at that moment I would never see him again. Deep down, I knew this day would come. My father slept on the couch as long as I can remember, and many times I

My mom in front of the Levittown house

was curled up in a corner listening to my parents fight. It was as if a piece of canvas was wrapped around my heart that day. Canvas is known for being durable and sturdy. These are the attributes I showed to the world. But I was forever changed, and it would take a lot to break though that tough fabric to my heart again.

After my dad disappeared, the house suddenly became peaceful.

My mom hadn't worked in 25 years. She didn't know where our dad was, nor when—or even if—he might come back. She literally had no idea where he went off to. My mother showed great courage. I am sure she had fear, anxiety, and uncertainty.

Unlike many kids of divorce, who still have their dads in their lives, I was left with no dad. I had no shared visits, no influence of a male role model. This would affect my relationships going forward. My fabric was ripped apart.

I found out much later that my dad left my mother with tremendous debt. She inherited his burden overnight. She got a job working as a secretary. She made only $3.25 an hour, but I felt rich for the first time in my life. We had clothing to wear and food in our bellies. And I felt safe.

Working on our home

(continued on page 52)

UNDERSTANDING TRENDS

The fashion designers create the trends, the couture. The style magazines like *Vogue and WWD* report on it. Then the trends are shown at the fashion shows in New York. They are fantasy to evoke a mood, and they need to be adjusted for regular life.

Designer manufacturers then adjust the trend for their customers. They manufacture the clothing out of the best, most luxurious fabric.

Next, "better "manufacturers adjust the trend for their customers. They copy the styles, but they make the clothes in less expensive fabrics.

Finally, the "moderate" manufacturers copy the trends. They're on trend, but they make the clothing out of very

inexpensive fabrics. The entire fashion industry is about replication. Imitation is the sincerest form of flattery, right?

WHEN TO BEND A TREND

When I was growing up, bell-bottomed pants, halter tops, and clogs were in. My youngest sister looked fantastic in them. Truth be told, she looked fantastic in anything.

But not *everyone* looks great in *all* trends. So, learn how to bend that trend. I teach my gals that just because it fits doesn't mean it *fits*. Clothes coming off the runway rarely look good in real life or are designed for you. The way to true style is knowing how to interpret the trends for your body shape and lifestyle. For example, if designers are showing a mini skirt, this can work great for you and become your focal piece— if you have great legs. Then bring it to real life by pairing it with chunky sweater, tights, and flats in winter or an easy top and flats in summer. It is all about being on trend—but not being too trendy. So, if your legs are not something you want to highlight, pick a different trend that highlights your slim waist. It is all about embracing yourself fully and loving the parts that are you.

The cityscape

Those childhood experiences of eating in the garage and going to bed with only bread and water are behind me now. But they became the thread in my pattern that led to my drive and success.

In our own ways, we all pitched in. Both my sisters and brother worked and contributed. House chores became my daily routine: vacuuming, loading the dishwasher, and cooking dinner before my mom got home. At age 13, I became a little adult.

We all took on mowing the lawn and house maintenance and improvement. My mom, sisters, and brother all pulled together to fix up our home. One day, a neighbor stopped by and said, "I didn't even recognize your house."

I remember taking the money I earned at my job when I was 14 to buy a painting for my mom to make our home better. It was a colorful cityscape. It made me feel good to contribute. That picture signifies our independence. It hangs above my mom's couch to this day.

About this time, I was left at home alone—a lot with my mom, brother, and sisters working. And my oldest sister married and moved out of the house. The silver lining to this was that I had the peace and quiet to reflect on who I was and where I wanted to be.

My youngest sister, Tracy

I was drawn to fashion even back then. As I grew up, my sense of style was influenced by my sisters, especially my youngest sister. I loved her cool style. She was very beautiful, and I idolized her. She was one of my many style influences. It was the seventies, so my sisters wore bell-bottoms and crop tops, clogs and halter tops.

I fondly remember learning disco steps with my sisters

BEAUTIFUL
INSIDE AND OUT

LET YOUR STYLE REFLECT RESPECT

I've worked since I was 14. I was fortunate to get a good job, and I believe it was because of how I presented myself. It got me further than my peers in their T-shirts. I dressed to reflect respect. Dress for the job you want.

Dressing well shows respect—for your job, for your position, and for yourself. Sadly, there's been a tectonic shift in our culture toward ultra-casual dressing.

One of my clients works for a large corporation. She was shopping at Frox, and I showed her some new dresses that I thought would be great for her office. She shook her head no and explained that her department had been directed not to dress that way anymore.

"It intimidates the customers," she explained.

No one's dressing up anymore—not for work, church,

in our living room. Disco music plays in my head now, thinking of the Bee Gees and empowering tunes by Diana Ross, Chaka Khan, and Cheryl Lynn. Today, our customer-models in my store's fashion shows stride down our runway to these anthems.

As teens, we wore clogs and bell bottoms, but in our younger years, our mom raised us very conservatively, which included all our attire. My sisters and I weren't allowed to

not even to dine at five-star restaurants. As a kid, when we went to New York to a Broadway show, we dressed in our Sunday best. Last year, I went to see *Hamilton*, and people were wearing Uggs and leggings! The casualness shocks and saddens me.

I think it's a respect issue. When you dress slovenly, you *feel* slovenly.

When you dress up, you feel good! You project more confidence, and that carries through to whatever you are doing.

Business dress

wear pants to school. Always the rebel, I'd take a pair of pants in a bag and change into them in the woods near school. When I was around 14 or 15, I began emulating what I saw in the magazines, such as *Elle* and *Vogue*. Their clothes were like art that you wore. I would page through fashion magazines and try to replicate those looks.

When I was 18, I got my first real job. Every week on payday, I would shop at Urban Outfitters, a local chain.

When I walked into the store, I felt inspired and swept away by the energy of that store. Urban Outfitters gave me something I had craved for a long time—a way to express myself. Their style was industrial chic—unique, urban, artsy. This style wasn't sold in department stores. It was different. It was me.

As a young girl, I felt so different from my family—from everyone really. As the youngest, I wore hand-me-downs, homemade clothes. As I grew up my clothing choices became a way for me to express my unique personality. I was starting my fashion journey. I was ahead of the curve even then. My clothing became my rebel call to be different, to set myself apart, and these themes were the seedlings of my future style.

When I was in high school, all my peers were thinking about college. In our faith, college wasn't encouraged. The thought was that this would indoctrinate us into other ways of thinking. Rather than taking the college prep classes I would have pursued, I chose the creative route. Somewhere deep in my soul, the vision of a big life was alive. I believed in the American dream that if you work hard, you can do anything—even if you're starting from nowhere. I wanted to live in New York City in a loft and pursue a fashion career. Your predicament doesn't determine your destiny. I wanted to grow into the person I was meant to be.

The Foundation Garments

RIGHT AFTER GRADUATING HIGH SCHOOL in 1984, I stared my journey into the fashion world–almost. I started working for my brother's copier company. One of the items they sold was a color copier. It was expensive and unpopular. I was determined to sell it. You could put photography paper in it and print pictures. I asked myself, *What kind of company needs a lot of photos?* I came up with a few ideas, but my best lead was a modeling agency called John Casablanca.

"You can use this copier to print your models' photos," I explained to the director.

I had come up with a way to show how the copier would benefit her agency, making a true connection with people as I was taught so many years ago. I put myself in her stilettos. She saw something in me, something that perhaps I didn't see in myself.

"I think you would be a good fit here," she said, and she offered me a position in sales.

She became one of the many mentors that was a thread of women through my life.

I worked my way up to the assistant director of the modeling agency—my golden ticket into the fashion world. I met with the models, helped them create their portfolios, and scheduled them for classes that would give them skills to get work. I discovered that I love helping people and connecting them with other people and opportunities. At the time, the industry did not represent women of all sizes and ages. This aspect did not sit well with me. It began my passion to help women of all ages and sizes feel beautiful.

What I did love was the fashion. I plastered photos of the great runway models all over my office. As I looked at those photos, I realized I wanted to make my own portfolio. I wanted to experience what my models were going through so I could understand them and help them. I was nervous because I had really never taken a good photo in

● Buttoned Up

UNDERSTAND YOUR CUS

Everything I ever needed to know about selling, I
learned early on. I learned that you have to put
yourself in your customer's shoes. You have to learn
what she needs, then provide it. Learn what her
problems are, then solve them.

I do this every day. I learn each Frox gal's who,
what, why, and how. When a customer walks into
Frox. I greet her warmly, then I ask about how she's
doing and who she is (learning her who). I ask what
she's looking for (learning her what). Then I ask
why she needs it (learning her why). Perhaps she's
having a great day because she's off from work,
shopping with her BFF. She needs to buy a dress
for her daughter's wedding next month. I've
assessed her body shape, ascertained her best
physical traits, and appraised her style (learning
how she looks best).

Now I know her who, what, and why, and how I can
show her the perfect dresses to suit her shape,
needs, and style.

the past. But I used an in-house photographer who was
kind and patient with me.

As I prepared for the shoot, I gathered all my coolest
outfits. We went to Philadelphia, to some of the most sce-
nic places in the city. It was a beautiful day, a little windy
but we ended up having a great shoot. I still have my port-

My portfolio pictures from the Philly shoot

folio and look back to a time when I was so new to the fashion industry and had so much to learn.

Today, we do many photo shoots for the Frox website and marketing. We make it a point to represent all women. With the ever-changing times, we have brought our online presence to a new level. As much as I enjoyed the job and my boss, I was looking for something else. I was in search of my life's purpose.

After my exposure to the world of fashion, I imagined moving to New York to work in the fashion world. I knew through it I was going to find my platform, with a message of empowerment. I wanted to help women believe in themselves like I was learning to do.

As I started to pursue future plans, I realized that because I didn't go to college my options were limited. For many years, that made me feel like I was not enough. That piece of paper? It was always the brass ring just out of my reach. I envied my friends and coworkers with college degrees. Years later, I would take college classes, and the overwhelming sense of accomplishment of just being able to walk through those classroom doors brought me to tears.

In my twenties, I decided to move out to an apartment in Fallsington, Pennsylvania, with a friend. We rented the third floor of the 300-year-old Stage Coach Tavern. It was built in the 1790s along the coach route. Over the years

The Historic Stagecoach Tavern

with numerous additions, it was used as a jail, post office, and hardware store. When we lived there, the first floor was set up as the tavern with furniture and props to create the scene as it would have been back then. The second floor housed the colonial re-enactment costumes for the annual Fallsington Day celebration. The third floor was our apartment with a very low ceiling pitched in the shape of the roof. Thank God we were short. We could not even put regular furniture in it. But it was both of our first apartment. I was really feeling my independence, but also fear and uncertainty. It was close to home but far away from the life I knew. I started to understand how my mom must have felt, all alone with new challenges to face when my dad left.

To support my new lifestyle—not to mention pay the rent—I needed gainful employment. So, I took a job as a cocktail waitress. This really led to a funny double life: I would show up for my weekly Bible meeting and then rush out to work at a bar where I wore a modified tuxedo with just briefs as a bottom. The bar was three stories high, so in heels I carried drinks on trays well above my head with droplets from the sticky sweet drinks dripping down my arm. It was quite a different experience than serving drinks to Nanny's friends when I was young. My life was compartmentalized. As a result, I was becoming really good at playing so many disparate roles.

FASHION FORWARD

One night at the bar, I met a creative go-getter like me. The man owned a company that made friendship bracelets out of ski rope. He had curly hair, and he was very tall and thin with long legs. He always told people that his long long legs were good to ski the moguls. He skied competitively and was training for the Olympics. He was selling the friendship bracelets in all the places he skied.

As we talked, he said he felt that I would be good at traveling and selling the bracelets in the mid-Atlantic region. This was new to me. I had sales experience, but I never traveled the road before. I needed to adapt to a completely different role. They say fake it until you make it. Boy, was I really faking it. This was a brand-new dyebath.

I took those bracelets to dozens of surf stores on the New Jersey and Maryland coastlines. I got to see beautiful scenery. There were many long car rides, lonely hotel nights, and meals alone. Many times, I was unsure of what the next day would bring, but I was open to new experiences.

I was surprised by how many stores I was able to place them in and how many opportunities this presented to me. The friendship bracelets were named Amigaz, which was a combination of French for friend and Spanish for Amigo.

So, as we would put the bracelet on someone's wrist, we would say, "French for friend is ami, and Spanish for amigo, put them together-AMIGAZ."

This was such a great way to connect with people; they loved it.

We got the bracelets into stores throughout the country. A local radio station WMMR loved them and gave one away every day.

But what was really amazing was that we were able to be a sponsor at the Amnesty International - Human Rights tour in 1988 at RFK stadium in Philadelphia. The concert was to educate and move a generation toward activism. The headliners were Sting, Bruce Springsteen, and Tracy Chapman. I will never forget being a part of the 75,000 people there. We were not there solely for the music; we were there to raise money for the hundreds of thousands being persecuted in Africa.

We went around the crowd spreading the message of peace and unity by putting friendship bracelets on anyone we could. We even got backstage, and I was able to put bracelets on Bruce Springsteen and Tracy Chapman. I always had the desire to do something bigger than myself.

The next opportunity that presented itself was being invited to share a booth at the trade show Action Sports Retailer in California. My boss's neighbor was the national sales manager for a surf company. He wanted to help us get exposure, and we were extra help in the booth—a win-win for everyone.

My boss decided to go to the show a few days before me to help set up the booth. I was nervous. I had never traveled across the country. I had to navigate the airport and overcome a complete fear of flying. I remember being overwhelmed by the amount of people in the airport. In my small-town life, I had never seen so many people in one place. I stepped on to that plane terrified, but I knew I had to have faith. The definition of faith is knowing that at our core, we are more than anything we will ever face. On the plane, I held tightly onto the arms of my seat, closed my eyes, and up we went. I was on my way to a new dyebath. I was excited to get there. At the time in the late 80s, the surf industry was booming. The manufactures went all out. Body Glove would rent out a bar, and we'd all dance to reggae music. Zinka sunscreen would have a VW bus with girls dancing on top painted with the colored sunscreen. Jimmy Z would pour sand on the convention floor and have many girls in bikinis showing off their wares. I wore the men's surf clothes I was selling, having adapted them to my small frame. I felt very overdressed compared with all the girls walking around in bathing suits.

Around that time, a friend told me about the funky town of New Hope, Pennsylvania. She loved working in a restaurant there and thought it would be a good fit for me. I left the bar cocktail waitressing because being in a revealing outfit and often getting grabbed, fending off improper comments, and even having my legs burnt with cigarettes because it was so crowded was starting to get old. I started waitressing and bartending in New Hope instead. This was a different scene than where I came from. The uniform was not revealing. It was a branded polo shirt and khaki shorts. There were no improper comments or being grabbed. It was a jazz club, and acts came from all around the country to play there. The bar was filled with an array of different people: artists, authors, and famous actors and actresses. They came to this oasis of a bar on the weekends because it was close to NYC. I also met famous activist Abbie Hoffman, who was a member of the Chicago seven. He would sit on the patio and tell us many stories about the 60s and how they changed the narrative in this country. I remember that my mother would also tell me about this tumultuous time. She said that is one of the reasons she became one of Jehovah's Witnesses. She felt at that time the world had gone mad. I loved being surrounded by all of these people who were creating and living their dreams.

During the day, I also worked as a sales associate at a boutique down the road from the New Hope bar. My bosses at the boutique were fun and eccentric. They had cool style and lived to the beat of their own drum. I had so many creative ideas that flowed through me as we merchandised the store, designed the windows, and created the displays. We had to be creative because the store was in an old Victorian home split up into retail on the bottom floors and apartments on the top floors. Just outside our doorway was an odd space next to the staircase. My boss decided to fill it with odd finds, skates, suitcases, trunks, lamps, etc. He painted them a slate blue that matched our store. The color created a symmetry between the items even though each was a different size and shape. I loved it, and it inspired my theme later on of making the ordinary extraordinary.

The boutique's first fashion show was at a local bar. It was packed; it felt like all of New Hope was there. The hair and makeup team styled me as a daytime Marilyn Monroe, with finger waves and long eyelashes. The stylist loved my bleached blonde hair. My hair and clothing still at this time was my way of expressing myself. It was all about personal expression—being unique and letting the world see it. We had worked on the show for months and months. I smile thinking about this now. One of my fellow workers begged to let us Vogue at the show. At that time Vogue-ing was the new dance craze. Malcolm McLaren had started it in all the gay clubs; Madonna went to one of them and adopted it for her audience. So, he would be in the store Vogue-ing and singing. It was great. We all loved it, but my boss would get frustrated and say, "No Vogue-ing in the store!" with a half-smile. Needless to say, my boss did not let us do it. Instead, we walked to all the 80s anthems. As I walked out, I was nervous because this was a completely new scene. But I drew on my experiences from the modeling agency, and my bosses were pleasantly surprised.

As I told my bosses stories of my religious background, one of them literally fell off his chair when I revealed that at age 24 I was saving myself for marriage. They were from the gay community and could not imagine my life. They were an inspiration in their dress but more importantly in how they seemed not to care what others thought of them. I envied that in them. I spent my whole life trying to please others and fit into a mold. They were so bold and courageous and a year or so later, when I was getting married, they came to my very conservative congregation and sat in the front row, knowing that some guests would not approve of their lifestyle. They showed up for me because they cared for me more than they cared for their own comfort. I was so grateful for their threads of love and support.

Just as I had settled into the groove of my New Hope life, my life took a hard turn. I learned that my father had died. I had not seen or heard from him for many years. It was if I had locked those emotions away in the back of my closet. But as I thought about going to his funeral, they came tumbling out.

My dad left when I was 13, so we never saw that part of the family tree. I had always felt different from my mom's side of the family. I never understood why I felt that way until I met my dad's family.

Oh, that side. That's where I come from, I thought.

All my dad's extended family lived in New York. They were funky, artsy, unique. I learned that one of my aunts owned a fabric company called Tiger Knitting Co. Meeting them, I discovered who I was and where I was from. It awoke aspirations in me to move to the big city live a life like they were and pursue a fashion career.

I was finally starting to see the fibers of the beautiful tapestry I was weaving.

CHAPTER 4

The Wedding Dress

I LOVED MY LIFE. I was working and pursuing many of my passions.

I certainly wasn't interested in dating. I was just returning from traveling across the country, attending all the surf trade shows, and having the time of my life. I had big, important plans for my future. In fact, I had recently sworn off men. Guess what happens when you're not looking?

One day, I was skiing with friends. I was dressed like a surfer chick, with friendship bracelets stacked all the way

Puffy pink ski suit

up my arm. I painted green Zinka on my nose, and I was wearing a puffy pink ski suit.

Even though I was wearing a puffy pink suit, I must have been projecting confidence. I wasn't looking for love, but I attracted it anyway.

I had bent over to fix my boot. Out of nowhere, a preppy guy came up and swooshed next to me in the snow. I was attracted to his boldness. I wanted to learn more. So, we spent the day going up and down the mountain getting to know one another. We started talking about my travel adventures. I learned we had a lot in common. We shared many of the same core values, because he was in the same faith as me. Yet he was different from many of the boys I had known. I liked the way he looked

BEAUTIFUL
INSIDE AND OUT

CLOTHE IN CONFIDENCE

Clothing can be empowering. When you feel beautiful, it can give you confidence. You project that to people effortlessly—with no work on your part. It's that *je ne sais quoi*—a pleasing quality that can't be described. You are captivating. Confidence is addictive. People want to be with people who have that air of ease, that charm.

at the world. He was everything I was looking for at the time. He worked in construction; he could build anything. I loved hearing him share all of his stories with me. I found myself falling in love and imagining this exciting new chapter in our lives. Our courtship lasted for less than a year. In that span, we experienced so many fun times. We went to restaurants and night clubs and took the top off my Jeep and drove down to the shore. Our family and friends liked each other, so we decided to tie the knot.

I imagined the life we would lead would be far different than the traditional background we both were raised in. We looked at our childhoods and wanted to do better in so many ways. We did not want to fall into

Our wedding day

the roles that were embedded in us. As we were taught, the man was the head of the house, and the woman had to submit. This certainly was not me. I wanted a partner and friend. He did not want to play this role either.

We were married on August 26, 1990. We had a

reception in a beautiful venue in New Hope. My husband and I danced in front of the crowd to dramatic operatic music, having recently taken dance lessons together. We enjoyed an elegant meal. The entire day was magical. It represented what I desired most, which a wedding that was inspired and expressed from all of my collective fashion experiences.

The wedding industry is a subset of the fashion industry, and I relished every second of wedding planning. At our rehearsal dinner, I wore my unique style: cowboy boots, Body Glove bike shorts, a Betsy Johnson bustier, and a Marc Jacobs double-breasted jacket. I held my white punk hair back with a black headband. I painted my lips a dramatic red. It was unconventional, but that's who I was—fashion forward.

At my wedding, I felt like a princess. I wanted it to be the high style I had seen in all the magazines. I wore a portrait-style gown with a pearl choker and the longest train I could find. In the nineties, Doc Marten shoes were popular, and I wore them all the time. Some friends peeked under my wedding dress, sure I would even wear them on my wedding day.

"I can be a lady for one day," I jokingly protested, showing off my delicate heels.

My six bridesmaids wore colors popular in that day—

Our wedding party

green dresses with pink roses—and matching portrait necklines. Getting those six perfect bridesmaids dresses was a challenge. I had to fit and flatter every kind of body shape you could imagine: tall, petite, curvy, athletic, and slim. Both apples and pears. It was a fruit bowl of shapes. The trick was getting two pieces. The top was a portrait neckline wrap jacket, which could accommodate all their bust lines. It cinched in at the waist to give them all a little shape. The bottom was a full-length straight skirt that skimmed over all their hips perfectly. This would be practice for all the future fittings I would do at Frox. My husband and his six groomsmen sported classic tuxes modeled after Gene Kelly—black and white tuxes with tails. Our pictures were taken at historic Font Hill in Doylestown, Pennsylvania. Again, my experiences at the modeling agency paid off, and our pictures were stunning. To this day, I love paging through the albums and looking at them. It was a fashion moment for sure.

We honeymooned in a quaint bed and breakfast in Cape May, New Jersey. It was a beautiful Victorian with yellow and green accents. It had great big porches, a library, and beautiful views. They served breakfast every morning with homemade signature granola, fresh fruits, and breads. Lots of older couples were staying there as well. As I look back, we were so young and still had so many things to experience. I laugh about it now. We did not use any of these amenities because we were so in love that we stayed in our room most of the time.

We have returned to that B&B on milestone anniversaries to enjoy all that they have to offer.

My husband and I had found an apartment together in Doylestown, Pennsylvania. We moved in together after our wedding day. We fixed up the old Victorian that was made into four apartments to resemble the New York apartments I so longed for. It had great wood floors, a fireplace, and high ceilings. We exposed the brick wall in

SHINE ON SPECIAL EVENTS

You know you're only going to wear your prom gown or wedding dress once. But when choosing an outfit for other special events, it's helpful to take a longer-term view of the purchase. If it's too dressy, you will get less wear out of it because it won't go to multiple places.

I teach my Frox girls to do this unconventionally. You want to feel amazing. Fit and drape are critical. I help people pick things that they can wear again. The cost per wear is better. You can choose a dress or outfit that's not one-time use but elevate it for the event with jewelry. This way you're not buying a dress for one occasion.

the kitchen. My husband painstakingly made a counter bar with a wine-and-glass rack that housed all the glassware from my bartending days. It was the start of our journey together. When I put on that white dress, I could not imagine the many dyebaths we would have to endure in the future. Our fabric is always being woven. My husband and I are still in a dyebath. Who knows how we will emerge, but we will be stronger and more resilient than we ever imagined we would be.

As we settled into our new life, I decided to look for more suitable work than bartending, so I went into a shop in Lahaska, Pennsylvania. As is my outgoing nature, I struck up a conversation with the owner. We discovered a mutual love of fashion.

"My sons own a clothing manufacturer in Plumsteadville" she said. "They need someone to answer the phone."

I thought, *I can answer the phone like nobody's business.* I am so glad I grew up in a time when you could try a job, see if you were good at it, and learn something new—without judgment or getting "off track."

At my interview with my future bosses, I knew if I wanted the job, I needed to dress for success. I really had no idea what I was going to be doing. I left myself open to a new experience.

(continued on page 82)

Buttoned Up
CARPE DIEM

Seize the day. My dad taught me that a job is not a job—it's an opportunity.

And in this new job, I found my calling. It spoke to me.

Much like picking a garment: You can tell when you look and feel good in something and it matches your style. It is important to grab those key pieces that speak to you. Seize that moment, buy that garment, because those will be the pieces you cherish and wear forever. They will also bring back memories of a time you just went for it.

Opportunities are all around us; we just need to train our eyes to see them. Some opportunities might seem small at first, but upon closer look you might see that you can expand it into a greater opportunity. I've done that with success often in my life, much like making a ball of yarn into a beautiful sweater.

I have many examples, but this is by far my favorite. I was attending the inaugural Fashions Night Out 2009 headed up by Anna Wintour and many others. The purpose of this event was to invigorate the New York retail economy by driving people into the stores at the height of the recession. To kick it off, they held a fashion show at Lincoln Center around the fountains. And I had tickets to go!

When we arrived, there were white chairs surrounding the fountain. It was beautiful. The models were doing a run through. Immediately I spotted Gisele Bundchen, and I knew it was going to be a great night. We made our way to our seats, and my friend elected to stay in hers! I thought, *No way am I staying here! I see some of my biggest fashion heroes only steps away. Take a small opportunity and make it big, right? Here I go!*

So, of course, the first person I walked up to was the most powerful woman in fashion: Anna Wintour, Editor-in-Chief of *Vogue*. Like I learned many years ago, make a connection and you can talk to anyone.

Having background information about the event, I walked right up to her and said, "Hello, Anna. I am a boutique owner. I would like to thank you for creating this event. The fashion industry needs you."

"Well, clap loudly, dear. Clap loudly," she replied in her distinctive accent.

That was one of the most exciting things to happen to me. Wait, there's more!

Next, I walked up to Tory Burch--another fashion hero of mine. Anyone who knows me knows I drip in Tory Burch. I love that she is a local girl from Valley Forge, Pennsylvania. Most importantly, she heads up a foundation that empowers women entrepreneurs. Again, using a mutual connection, I walked up to her and said, "I am a boutique owner as well. We're both Philly girls, and I so appreciate the work you do for fellow entrepreneurs like me."

She thanked me and said, "So nice to meet you." OMG! Someday I would like to work for her foundation; it would be a dream come true.

Lastly, I walked up to yet another fashion hero, Diane von Furstenberg, who came up with the concept of the wrap dress. I also admire her work in empowering women.

I walked up to her and commented that I was a fellow woman in fashion and how much I enjoy her work. She thanked me, and we all scrambled to our seats. All this happened because I just went for it.

I was hired to do their customer service, but I took on many roles. I learned about drape, fabrication, garment dye, costing, customer service, shipping, getting samples to the salespeople, and eventually selling the garments. I relished in doing so many things. It served me well.

Little did I know then that it was going to be the best education I could have ever wanted. I was about to learn everything I needed to know about the fashion industry. Many things I learned, I still use to this day. It was a great foundation for all my future success.

This is where I got my *actual* education of dyebaths.

My new bosses were getting to know me, and I was getting to know them. They were brothers, and their mother was the shop owner who had directed me to them, and also the designer of the line they made, which was called No Saint. Their mother became another woman in my life to inspire and mentor me. I loved her style; she had short, grey hair cut into a pixie. She wore funky glasses and lots of black textured tunics, wide-leg crop pants, and of course great shoes. The family was from Austria, and the line had a European flair. She would teach me so many things about the industry.

I was the one they used in fit meetings, which is when the garments are tried on and perfected before they go into production. I soaked in everything in those meetings. I learned how fabric drapes over the body. How seams can give shape to the body. We also would do knit downs for the sweaters. A knit down is a square of knitted fabric in its raw state that you put into a dyebath to see how it affects the fabric. You can make many different effects like using a large knit and using heat shrinking it down to a smaller interesting knit. A great effect is using cotton and polyester twisted together. When you put them in a dyebath, the dye seeps into the cotton and rolls off the polyester giving a snowflake affect.

We were like mad scientists playing with color and texture—and of course playing with those funky buttons that adorned the sweaters.

Soon the owner trusted me enough to take me to the trade shows and show me how she bought for her store. Today I make sure I take my Frox employees to the shows to help them understand the industry and gain product knowledge. I want to be a mentor to my girls just like she was a mentor to me. The career path I wanted to be on was becoming clear to me, and I was willing to do the hard work to blaze that trail. I knew if I could believe it, I could create it.

FASHION FORWARD

INVESTMENT DRESSING: CLASSIC WHITE SHIRT

A white shirt is a wardrobe staple. Expect to spend. This is an investment piece—something that you will have in your closet for many years to come.

Here's what to look for:

- Crisp, white cotton
- Traditional styling, which means classic men's wear inspiration
- A layering collar
- Good buttons, such as tortoiseshell, gold, or silver
- French cuffs, which are taken from men's wear again and give an elevated look to the shirt

INVESTMENT DRESSING: CLASSIC BLACK PANTS

What to wear with that classic white shirt? Classic black pants, of course. Here's how:

- Fit is the most important.
- It must drape over the body for easy movement and be proportioned for the jacket or top you are wearing.
- The best fabric choices are gabardine or a Lycra/cotton blend.
- If you're an apple (you carry your weight in your belly), try cigarette pants to accentuate your legs.

- If you're a pear (you carry your weight in your bottom or legs), go for a straight leg.
- If you're petite, avoid a wide leg and choose a cropped pair.
- If you're tall and skinny, consider cigarette pants or wide legs.

CHAPTER 5

The Tailored Outfit

IN 1990, I WAS NEWLY MARRIED, with a new job I loved. I was happy. I was content.

Kind of. My feet were itchy. I wanted to spread my wings. The cliché is that opportunity knocks. Apparently, sometimes it also calls.

I was sitting at my desk in Pennsylvania. My bosses were in New York City at a trade show. They called in a panic.

"Jill, can you bring the salesman samples up to us?" one of my bosses asked, clearly distraught. "The samples weren't ready in time for the show setup."

The Javits Center

In the garment industry, samples are just that: a sample of the garments they hope to sell.

"Of course!" I answered cheerfully. I had gone to New York when I worked for the surf company. We attended surf shows at the Javits Center. So, I knew where they were. I had built some confidence, but I was still nervous because I didn't

New York skyline   *The trade show floor*

want to disappoint my new bosses. I knew I could figure it out. I drove to the blip of a Pennsylvania town called Tamaqua to pick up the samples at the dye house. I tossed the sweaters into a hockey bag, then I caught a train to the city.

On the two-hour train ride, I began to imagine what would happen next. I had been to the city many times before on our annual Broadway trips as a child, so I was comfortable there. I longed to get to know the city better—to feel at home in the Big Apple. I wanted a big life in the Big Apple.

And so, with dreams of a bigger life in my head, the ride to the city flew by. Like a NYC native, I hailed a cab to the trade show. Breathlessly, I raced to the No

KNOW YOUR FRUIT

The outfit I wore to the show was the right choice for my figure type. I'm what the fashion world calls an apple. I wore a long top skimming over my full belly, paired with leggings to accentuate my great legs, works for me.

Are you an apple or a pear? Some women carry their weight in their stomach and have thin legs: apples. Other

Saint booth and delivered the samples to my bosses.

I seized my chance to experience the trade show. I looked around me—the hustle and bustle of buyers and vendors animatedly showing their collections, and expressing opinions. They looked so smart in their trendy clothes—black and svelte, the unofficial "uniform" of NYC.

I had known this, of course, and dressed the part. My bosses had asked me to wear their earthy, hippie-chic clothing to the show. It wasn't exactly my usual punk New Hope

women carry weight in their bottoms or legs and have thin torsos: pears.

What to wear if you're an apple: Accentuate your legs with a fitted skirt or pants. Disguise your belly with a looser, flowing top.

What to wear if you're a pear: Accentuate your waist with a belt. Choose a fitted top to show off your slim stomach. Then let soft fabric drape over your hips with a wider-legged pant or dress.

style. I found an outfit that suited my style. As I settled into the show, I felt comfortable, in my element, home.

The trade show was very busy that day. As usual, it was filled with hundreds of manufacturers' booths. Their booths were lavishly decorated in the aesthetics of their line. The sales reps were posted out in front of their booths, smiling and engaging the buyers who walked through the show, aisle by aisle. In the in the industry, the title Sales Representative is shortened to Sales Rep. Also, the act of selling is sometimes called repping. When a buyer stopped by, the sales rep would show off the clothing—all the pieces together made that season's line. As you walked the rows, trends emerged: *Cropped sweaters are hot! Nautical is in! Camel is the new black!*

As buyers selected the clothes, the sales reps took their orders, which later that day were totaled, then passed along to the manufacturer, who fulfilled the orders. Millions and millions of dollars changed hands that day.

This day, the show was really hopping. The owners realized I was a new set of hands.

"Stand behind the girl showing the sweaters," my boss directed.

I took my post, and the girl started throwing sweaters at my feet! She'd show a buyer a sweater, then drop it behind her. *Clink* went some of the funky buttons that adorned their clothes when they hit the concrete trade show floor.

I quickly ascertained my new job was to pick up the sweaters, fold them, and return them to their spot on the shelves at the back of our booth.

I can do this! I thought. Never one to be idle, I began listening to what the sweater girl was saying. One of the owners noticed how quickly I was catching on and how intently I was paying attention to the sweater girl's sales presentation to the buyers.

"I think you could sell those sweaters," the owner said to me.

I think I can, too, I thought. I stepped up next to the sales rep and began talking to buyers who visited our booth.

I sold so many sweaters at that trade show, the brothers offered me a job as a sales rep. At the time, they had one sales rep who serviced New York and another who serviced New England. The brothers offered me my own territory, the mid-Atlantic territory of Pennsylvania and also New Jersey, Maryland, and Washington, DC.

I was ecstatic—though I was nervous and concerned that I didn't know the area. My can-do spirit jumped in. These were the days long before Waze and GPS, so I had to plot my route on actual paper maps. I knew I had to stay focused on my inner compass as well.

I began to venture out—to neighboring Bryn Mawr, then to Philadelphia, then to Allentown, and New Jersey. The farther I went, the better I felt.

It was 1998. I drove a sporty, maroon Jetta. I felt like a clown in a clown car. I had so many samples and the smallest car. I arranged my sample sweaters in big, blue garment bags. One day, in Ocean Grove, New Jersey, I was carrying my garment bags slung over one shoulder into a store.

(continued on page 96)

FASHION FORWARD

BECOME SWEATER SAVVY

Who doesn't love sweaters? Cozy, warm, soft, they remind us of crisp nights watching a football game under the lights or romantic evenings by the fireplace. Sweaters can accentuate your best features.

- To play up your bust line, choose a V-neck or sweetheart neckline.
- To show off a swan-like neck, try a cowl neck.
- Crew necks are harder to wear because they cut your line.
- If you are an apple, a soft sweater to drape over your belly is best. Longer is better; aim for a sweater that hits below your waist.
- For pears, consider a shorter length that hits at the waist to bring the focal point up to your face and away from the hip area.
- Choose a natural fiber sweater, such as 100 percent cotton or cashmere. They breathe better and are more sustainable than synthetics. Avoid poly blends. As you wash them, the poly rolls off the natural fibers, creating unsightly pills.

Sweater sets are a classic preppy look. They are generally crew neck because you can layer them. They are classics, and they really never go out of style.

To care for your sweaters—and other delicate items—wash them in cold water on the gentle cycle and place them flat to air-dry on a sweater drying rack. Soap and water won't hurt most fabrics, but heat will break down the fibers.

Avoid dry cleaning as much as possible. I don't buy—or sell— anything that requires dry cleaning. It's wasteful, and it kills the planet. Plus, it adds to your cost per wear. If you wear a garment 10 times, and every time you wear it, you spend $10 to dry-clean it, add $100 to the cost of that item!

A good sweater should last for many years.

Bruce Springsteen and his wife, Patti Scialfa, were shopping outside at the boutique next door.

"Those look like body bags," Bruce Springsteen said, jokingly.

Believe it or not, it wasn't the first time I heard this.

"No dead bodies. Just clothes," I quipped and ducked into the store.

At the time, I didn't know anything, I didn't know anyone, so I just drove around looking for stores. This was long before the internet; there was nothing to Google. I spent hours upon hours driving the towns of Pennsylvania, New Jersey, Maryland, and DC looking for clothing stores. To achieve my goals would take grit, hard work, and hustle.

When I found a store, I knew it wasn't wise to stride in and ask to speak with the owner. I knew intuitively that would be disruptive. Instead, I went in casually, checked out the store and their style, smiled and said hello to the sales gals, and took a business card off the counter. Then from home, I'd call and ask to speak with the owner or buyer, saying, "I have a new clothing line that would hang well with…" inserting something I had noticed in the store. More often than not, they'd reply, "Yes! I'd love to see it."

I discovered my knack for selling. I knew what it felt like to put myself in someone else's shoes. I was able to quickly discover what they wanted—what they needed.

CLOTHING CONNECTS US

Clothing is so much more than fabric to keep us warm and dry. Clothing is a powerful force, connecting us to many things:

- **Nature:** Various natural fabrics like cotton and linen and accents such as tortoiseshell and metal ground us and connect us to nature.

- **Culture:** The clothing we wear helps us to identify with and connect with our culture. Consider the sari, kimono, and kilt.

- **Our groups and organizations:** Uniforms and clothing identify us as part of a group or organization, such as rabbis in prayer shawls, monks in robes, and soldiers in camouflage.

- **Our past:** When you wear a piece of clothing, does it remind you of another time and place? Perhaps a T-shirt you got at a concert transports you back to that event. Or a cozy sweater you wore on your first date with your spouse reminds you of your love.

We are all interwoven, and our clothing plays a special role in that.

BEAUTIFUL
INSIDE AND OUT

INVEST IN QUALITY

Quality matters. Have you ever splurged on a really fine piece of clothing, such as a cashmere sweater or a pair of linen pants? Putting that garment on makes you feel like a million bucks.

On the other hand, have you ever tossed on a piece of off-the-rack clothing from a big box store? You know it was inexpensive, and it looks inexpensive.

Clothing manufacturing is a lot like baking: If you start with quality ingredients, you'll get a quality cake—or in this case, clothes.

Here are some tells of inexpensive clothing:

- Prints not lining up at the seams
- Buckling, loose, or crooked seams
- Plastic zippers
- Synthetic fabrics like polyester

That brings us to another problem with buying throwaway clothing: It ends up in landfills. Synthetic fabrics like nylon, polyester, and rayon can take many years to break down. It's ironic that they last for weeks or months in your closet—but they linger for generations

Then I tailored my presentation to match. It worked.

I got those sweaters into some of the best stores in the country. I couldn't believe it when I landed an appointment with Anthropologie—my dream store. I shopped there for

in the landfill. Now the fashion industry is beginning to do reverse cycling: transforming polyester clothing into plastic water bottles.

Quality clothing is all about the fabric. Natural fibers like cotton and linen breathe. Especially for menopausal women, who have their own personal summer, that's important. Linen is a beautiful choice. Yes, it wrinkles; embrace the wrinkles. You can steam them out, or choose a linen with a little rayon that helps with the drape.

On the other hand, synthetic fabrics like polyester are made of plastic. Much like wearing a Hefty bag, they do not breathe.

Did you know most people wear 20 percent of their clothing 80 percent of the time? For those pieces you wear often, it's worth the investment to buy quality garments.

Ironically, a quality garment will wear better, wash better, and last longer—maybe even 10 times longer— than an inexpensive one. Inexpensive fabric might look acceptable on the store shelf, but after washing, it often fades, pulls, or shrinks. Not every piece of clothing in your closet needs to be designer quality. But rather than buying 10 inexpensive shirts, invest that money in one nice top. Invest in quality; invest in you. You're worth it!

many years. I knew their merchandise inside and out. I understood and shared their unique point of view—fun, artsy, and inspiring. From all my years in sales, I knew that you always had to have a connection with the person you will be working with. I was sure I could make that connection. So, when another retailer I was working with pointed at a shirt I was showing and said, "This looks so Anthropologie," I got the idea to approach them by mentioning what she had said. I did my research and found out the buyer's name. I called her. "I was showing another retailer my line, and she felt that this line is a perfect fit for you," I said. She replied. "Well, I guess I have to see it,"

We made arrangements to meet. Their headquarters was on Walnut Street in Philadelphia. The architecture was amazing, and the building was known for its artistic, inspiring window displays. The old building had five half-circle steps leading to the grand entrance.

Back then, I transported my clothing line with a rolling rack—a clothing rack on wheels. I'd put the clothing into four big blue garment bags, then I'd hang the bags on the rack. Getting my rolling rack up those imposing stairs was a challenge. As I stood at the bottom of the stairs with my samples, it might as well have been Mount Fuji. I tried to wheel the rack through the city streets and attempt the stairs. Of course, it fell over. Classic rookie move for a sales rep. Resigned, I took my garment bags off the rack, hauled them up the steps one at a time on my back, tossed them on to the floor inside the entrance with a loud thunk! Then I hauled the closet-sized rolling rack up the stairs, and reas-

Buttoned Up

SOLVE YOUR CUSTOMERS' PROBLEMS

Again, my early years came into play in my life. I had overcome my fear of speaking to people. I knew instinctively how to relate to my buyers. And at the end of the day, sales is solving a problem or filling a need. You just need to think of how your product can do just that for someone. Later, when I opened Frox, I applied the same principles. People buy from someone they know and trust. So, when selling, know your product inside and out. Know your customers inside and out. And be a problem solver. If you help your potential customers achieve their goals, you will have much greater success. It is always about *them*—not about you.

sembled the whole thing inside. I'm sure I was a sight to behold! But it was time to suit up and show up. Which I did! The buyer gave me a test order for all 300 stores at that time. Courage is being afraid and doing it anyway. If I had never tried, I would have never gotten that order.

In addition, I canvased the mid-Atlantic, which meant driving my little Jetta through many states day and night. I was traveling to Washington DC and every little suburb in between selling my line of clothing. I was staying with a girlfriend, who was an intern at the White House. After my

Buttoned Up

DO WHAT YOU LOVE

I remember my mentors called it relationship sales. You don't really sell anyone anything. You're selling yourself. I took their advice when I opened Frox.

For me, it's all about the story. I'm a great story-teller, but more importantly, I'm a great listener. Some customers are not used to being pampered, but that is what you are there for: to make them feel heard and understood. I ask my gals questions to learn about their wants and needs, their family, their job, and who and where they want to be in life. My relationships with my Frox gals are really close. My closest friends are all also some of my clients.

Clothes shopping is an intimate experience. Women are exposing their fears about their bodies. They're getting undressed and redressed in a fitting room. They come out to show me the clothing. I help them trust me. They know I will make them feel great and wonderful.

long day driving around DC and surrounding areas, she asked me to pick her up at work so we could go back to her home. I drove around and around, trying to find her building, but all the buildings were white.

Where was THE White House? I wondered.

Finally, I called her to find out where she was. "You can find all your little stores, but you can't find The White

House. Do you watch the news?"

My friend is another powerful woman who certainly threaded through my life. I knew her at the start of her journey at the White House, but her achievements are astounding.

I laughed and realized I had a long way to go to lose my small-town roots.

As a sales rep, I got to see all sides of the fashion industry. I saw what resonated with store buyers—and what didn't. I organized and hung hundreds of samples in preparation for my road trips. I continued to grow my repping business by taking on new lines and going to more trade shows. Along the way, I met women buyers who inspired me by their wisdom, experience, and willingness to mentor me. I still use their advice to this day.

I was gaining momentum, which was tapping into my potential and fueling belief in myself. I know that if I was not growing, I was dying. The universe had a plan for me greater than I could imagine.

It was whispering to me, *More. More. You deserve more.*

But if you don't listen to the universe, the volume turns up. Finally, God screams: *Pursue your dreams.* I had to give myself the permission to be wildly successful.

CHAPTER 6

The Business Suit

**I SALES REPPED FOR THE CLOTHING MANUFAC-
TURER FOR ABOUT SIX YEARS.** While I enjoyed it, in
time it began to feel limiting. I began to consider taking a
leap to go out on my own and become an independent sales
rep. This was an exhilarating—but scary—proposition. I'd
lose the safety net a full-time position offers: a steady
income. But I'd gain freedom, the opportunity to sell other
lines, and limitless potential!

Sometimes you have to trust your parachute and jump.
In 1996, I jumped.

My company needed a name. I used to joke that I sell

frocks—an old-fashioned term for women's dresses. Turning that word on its side a bit, I called my business *Frox*.

I was an independent sales rep, so I could pick and choose which clothing lines I wanted to sell. You don't want to put all of your shirts in the same shopping basket. I picked up a line called Aly-Wear, which at the time was one of the top selling clothing lines in the country. I picked up three or four other lines as well.

Now that I was an independent sales rep, I was competing against hundreds of other clothing reps. I needed to hustle more than ever. Schlepping my rolling rack in the back of my Jetta wasn't working for me anymore.

I upgraded to a mobile showroom—a white 24-foot RV outfitted with racks, a couch, and a table. The one I purchased was older because I could not afford a new one. It broke down more than it ran, it seemed. I felt like part-time sales rep and part-time diesel mechanic.

The many times I was broken down on the road waiting for a tow truck, I wanted to give up. I often wondered if there was an easier way to make a living. But my passion always won out.

The mobile showroom opened up my world. I could transport so many more samples now—which meant I could show several clothing lines rather than just one.

I was opening up to all the new experiences presenting themselves to me. It is like mordanting fabric, which is using a substance to open up the fibers so it can receive the dye.

As an independent sales rep, I could travel anywhere my RV could take me. I continued to focus on my clients

 # Buttoned Up

MAKE YOUR CUSTOMERS' LIVES EASIER

Go out of your way to make life easy for your customers. When I was starting out, I transported my clothing samples in garment bags on a rolling rack. This meant I needed to roll everything into a store to show the buyer or owner. I was going into *their* space, where they were swamped with work, distractions, stress. That buyer has a million things going on, so I need to make her job as easy as possible.

I invested in a mobile showroom so that I could make meeting with me easier and more pleasant for buyers. They would come out to my showroom, getting a little break from their store. I designed my showroom to be comfortable and relaxing. I used colorful carpets, high-quality slipcovers, and matching curtains. The buyers and owners could sit at the table or on the couch. I offered them a beverage and a snack. They could focus on me and my line—a welcome diversion from their store.

Buttoned Up

CLOSE THE LOOP

Always follow through. Be the person your customers can rely on to go the distance.

In the fashion industry, once a sales rep makes the sale, her job isn't done. It might be tempting to trust that the manufacturer is going to do what they're supposed to: make and ship the clothing to fill the order. But things don't always go as planned. Sometimes an order doesn't go through, a shipment slips through the cracks, or a dye bath goes south.

I made it my business to circle back and ensure the manufacturer shipped the products on time. Then I confirmed the customer received the order and everything was perfect. Going the extra mile to close the loop helped me to identify and even anticipate problems. This earned me lots of repeat business—stores that ordered from me season after season, year after year.

and contacts in Pennsylvania, New Jersey, Maryland, and DC. I had worked hard to build these relationships. My store buyers knew that I would take care of them. I always emphasized the importance of our relationship over the quick sale.

These women showed me the journey they were on and the choices they made along the way and how I learned from their mistakes and triumphs. As I worked with them for many hours in my mobile showroom, weaving together our collective experiences, I knew this was so much more than buying clothing for the season.

Being an independent sales rep also allowed me to work with several designers—not just one.

I enjoyed our national sales meetings where sales reps from around the country would meet, all in our varying style of dress: east coasters in their urban black "uniform," west coasters in casual looks, and sales reps from everywhere in between. It was also exciting to meet the designers of the line as they unveiled this season's inspirations. We would sit in a room, all of us creatives spinning our ideas together, with the collaboration making an even better collection. It was much like when three pieces of yarn are spun together, making a much stronger garment.

Meeting and working with these buyers, sales reps, and designers continued the thread of empowered women through my life.

Working as a sales rep, each day was a unique adventure for me. Usually, I had several appointments a week. Most days, I would start very early and come home very late.

While I had enjoyed my bohemian life traveling all

FASHION FORWARD

DARE TO BE DIFFERENT

I repped up to three weeks before my kids were born. Even as a young mom, I liked to set myself apart by dressing differently than my peers—ahead of the fashion curve. Even now in my adult life, I dress very differently than all my friends. The husband of one of my friends jokes, "I don't understand what you're wearing. But because you're wearing it, it must be a thing. Is it a thing?"

"Yes, it's a thing," I answer. "You'll see—in a year or two."

How can you be ahead of the fashion curve? Watch the fashion shows online, pay attention to magazines like *Vogue*, and shop in fashion-forward stores like Frox.

over four states, I knew I could not keep up this pace if I were to have children.

Our daughter was born in 1996. Having a baby truly changes everything. It was both an exciting time and a frighting time, learning many new things about life. My copy of *What to Expect When You're Expecting* was tattered and torn from me reading and taking notes almost every day. But when I looked at my perfect baby girl, I knew everything would be okay. I also already was imagining how I would introduce her to the fashion world, how I would dress my baby girl in all the coolest styles. I thought

Me and my kids

to myself, *When she turns 16, I am going to take her to Paris, and we will see great fashion together.* When she turned 16, we did!

Then in 2000, my son arrived. He arrived quickly. I went into labor at 12 pm. I learned that is absolutely the worst time to go into labor. Everyone is ready to take you to the hospital in the middle of the night. But at 12 pm everyone I knew was at work, including my husband. So, I called our babysitter, who worked at our day care center.

"Can you take me to the hospital? No one is around to help me," I asked.

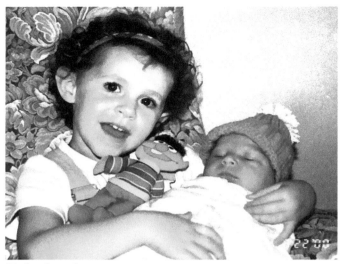

My daugther and son

"Well, I have a lunch break. I can take you, but I will have to leave right away." She said. Off we went to the local hospital. I was having contractions going up in the elevator. She was young. I am sure she was scared to death as she most likely had never seen this in action. She left me. I was all alone. I thought, *I have done this before. I can do it again.*

I put my feet up in the stirrups and said, "Give me the ice chips. Let's go"

I was ever the firecracker, just like in my youth. My son was born in 45 minutes. My husband barely made it. He got to my hospital room just in time to cut the cord.

Soon after my son was born, my life—like so many people's lives—took a hard turn.

September 11, 2001, started just like any other day. I got up, drank my coffee to clear the sleep from my brain, checked my calendar to plan my route, and confirmed my samples were all organized and ready to show. I looked forward to a perfect day, traveling through fall foliage-adorned back roads north to Allentown then on to Stroudsburg, Pennsylvania.

At my Allentown stop, the owner looked pale as he came out to my mobile showroom. "Something just happened in New York," he said. "I think you might want to go home to be with your family."

A little confused, but undaunted, I headed to my next appointment in Stroudsburg, when the owner called.

"I can't see you today because of what happened in New York," she said.

I had no idea what they were talking about because I had left very early that morning and hadn't listened to any news. My manufacturers and friends started calling me because I travel to all three of the cities where planes crashed: New York, Washington, DC, and Somerset County, Pennsylvania. Nobody knew what was going on. I remember thinking, *Are they going to hit the Liberty Bell next? What monuments are they planning to crash next?* There was so much uncertainty. In my reflections, I think that we were so innocent at that time.

At that, I turned around and drove home. I turned on the TV and realized the world had just changed. I would have to pivot. I found myself back in the dyebath.

CHAPTER 7

The Button

I WATCHED MY BELOVED NEW YORK CITY BURN.
My heart ached for New Yorkers—those who were lost, those who lost loved ones, those who lost livelihoods.

As much as I longed to live in the city, as much as I loved to go there, a lot of the luster rubbed off the Big Apple for me that day. Like for so many, travelling at all lost its appeal. It was nerve racking when we did our first show only weeks after the terrorist attacks. We would hear military planes flying over the Javits Center. It was still a no-fly zone at the time. At every tunnel, I was asked to step out while they inspected my mobile showroom searching with mirrors under it to see if I was carrying bombs. I

Buttoned Up

DESIGN A GREAT LOGO

If a picture is worth a thousand words, a logo is worth a thousand pictures. A logo is the highly concentrated, intensely powerful symbol of your business. Choosing a logo is one of the most important business decisions you will make.

No pressure.

When designing my logo for Frox, I knew it had to be a button. Buttons symbolized my beginning in the fashion world. I chose the classic four-hole button. My purpose in choosing the button as my logo is that when someone buttons up their shirt, I want them to think of Frox. I want them to think of me.

joked, "Nope, only sweaters." I don't think they found it funny. It was a crazy time.

I remember being evacuated more times than I can count. When I was visiting stores in New Jersey and asking how they were doing, they would answer, "We are selling a lot of black suits."

Shortly after, there where copycat shootings in the parking lot of shopping centers in my territory. A week or so after, my buyers understandably were nervous to come out to the mobile showroom, so I pulled up to the door, and they quickly jumped in. We were working inside, forgetting the outside world for a bit. One day, a knock on the door startled us. It was the police asking us to step out so they could search the truck. This happened often, because the terrorist used a white box truck, and my mobile showroom was a big white truck. After that I thought, *It is not worth it to risk my life to sell sweaters.*

Home was the only place that felt truly safe. I thought, *I want to open a shop a block from my home and be close to my children. If anything happens again, I can close the door and be with them,* I decided.

Right after 9/11, I knew in my heart the best decision for me was to open my own store. I was not able to go to NYC right then, but I could bring NYC to my little corner of the world. When you really want something and work toward it, all the universe conspires in helping you achieve it.

In earnest, I began to plan. The name, of course, would be Frox—because the store had grown out of my experience sales repping all those years. I didn't have to think long for my logo. For me it had all started with a button—the many buttons on those No Saint sweaters dropped at my feet so long ago by the sweater girl at the NYC trade show.

Original storefront

I found the perfect location. It was a 100-year-old building on a quaint side street in the Norman Rockwell–like town of Perkasie, Pennsylvania. Back then, it was a small, small town. The town center consisted of a gas station, a yoga studio, and a toy shop. There was not much else in the towns surrounding it for miles. Clearly there was an opportunity here.

Could I take this concept and idea and make it into a thriving business? I had a picture in my mind of the entire store, so it was just a matter of buttoning everything up.

I hoped to build a place where women would feel special and empowered and knowing Frox was a place to call home. My "Aha" moment happened when I signed my daughter up for gymnastics class. We were new to the town,

Storefront today

and I thought it would be a fun thing for her to do. The class was held in a loft space that had a very high, steep staircase. All the mothers stood on the stairs waiting for class to begin. I had my daughter on my hip, and I thought we would all tumble down those steps. I dropped my daughter off and went down the steep staircase. I thought, *Ok how am I going to kill an hour? There must be other mothers like me looking for things to do. There's nothing to do in town.*

The store in progress

Then I saw the space that would soon become my shop. I fell in love with the building the moment I saw it, though it needed a lot of attention. The walls had shown years of use. The plaster was cracked and was sponge painted an odd color of green. It had an old furnace and no air-conditioning. It didn't even have a bathroom!

But it had beautiful architecture. My eyes were immediately drawn to the tin ceiling and the wood floors, and I knew I had found my store. It had good bones. The outside of the building was brick. It was midway in a row of stores.

The storefront had deep windows. They were perfect for displays like the ones I loved so long ago on our yearly trips to Broadway. Already, I could picture the displays I would create there. I was going to bring New York to Perkasie!

I had a clear vision of what I wanted Frox to be. After all, I had visited hundreds of stores as a sales rep. I had seen the best of the best, and I cringed remembering the worst of the worst. I could picture Frox in my mind—the colors, the fixtures, the look, and the feel.

We fully renovated the inside of my new store. My husband's talents helped to transform the space into something truly spectacular. I thought, *It's got to look good, feel good, smell good, and be like nothing they had seen before.*

We prepped the plaster walls, and then he painted them goldenrod yellow. I wanted my customers to feel warm and welcome in my store.

I used local artists wherever I could. I hired one to stencil inspiring words all around the top walls. Some of the words that encircle the store are Love . . . Dream . . . Inspire . . . Believe . . . Bliss . . . Hope . . . Reflect . . . As I look at these words every day, it reminds me of the reason I

Buttoned Up

CREATE A VISION BOARD

For many years, I've had a vision board. On it, I post pictures or drawings of things that I want to have in my life. My first vision board was all about Frox. My second vision board featured this book, a picture of me speaking on a TED stage, and a picture of my dream home. Everything on my vision board has come true, so I'm making a bigger vision board.

Most people create their vision boards on poster board and hang them. I personally like my vision board to be more private—and portable. So, I'm creating this one in an 8.5 by 11-inch notebook. I look at it every night—to remind myself of my dreams and to reinforce them. Each time I look at it, my dreams feel closer to reality.

On the first page of my new vision book, I wrote, "If the version of you from five years ago could see you right now, she'd be so proud!" I have an overall vision: "I decided to start living the life I imagined. It's already yours." I added pictures of this book and my family. Another page features books that inspire me. A third page is all the people I want to meet from my speaking: Lisa Nichols, Brené Brown, and Oprah. I also have a photo of the day I met Jack Canfield. The

opened the store: to bring beauty love and inspiration to all who walk through the doors.

I wanted Frox to feel like home, so every day, we light candles. Our signature scent wafts through the air—spar-

caption I wrote says, "Speak it into existence." Next, I'm going to do a page about travel abroad and a new page about Frox.

To make your vision board, cut out pictures and words from magazines, print them from the internet, or even draw them. Then attach them to a piece of poster board and hang it somewhere you'll see it often. Or like me, put it in a notebook A vision board is a powerful visual reminder of what you are hoping to attract to your life.

kling citrus, creating energy and happiness in the store.

The floor of the building was a beautiful blonde wood. The distressed planks told the stories of the many people who walked through this space. I have been told it was once a Five & Dime store, and residents remember buying penny candy and walking on the creaky floors. The ceiling was an intricate patterned tin. Although it was dirty, I could see its former glory coming through.

We installed industrial hardware throughout. My husband built the counter custom fit for all the supplies it would hold, and he hand-hammered tin as the top. As he did this, I envisioned all the conversations and clothing that would pass over this counter. Above, tin lanterns cast a warm, soft glow.

On the ceiling, we installed large schoolhouse lights. I was told later by a life-long resident that those were the original style lights she remembered from her youth. We kept the history, but updated it, too. My inspiration was Anthropologie, the store I sold to many years before. I always loved the unique, unexpected ways they created displays.

I remember some of my first displays. I would visit the antique store across the street and find unique items. Once I used a large flour sifter for an earring display. We had an old pie cupboard for a candle display. I stacked terra cotta pots for shoe stands, filled funky plates and dishes with rice and beans, and placed jewelry on them. Whenever I had a crazy idea for a window, I would run over excitedly and ask, "Do you have…" Irons, yarn spools, vintage books, spinning wheels, crates, you name it, she had it. She would think for a moment, smile, and say, "I think I have it. Let me dig around a bit."

I think she secretly loved being part of the excitement and finding us a trove of treasures.

I was so grateful for my husband's construction background, which he had hinted at so long ago on that ski slope.

Rather than buying commercially made racks and fixtures, I commissioned a local artist to hand forge them. We visited his shop to see how they were made. He does it just like colonial times with an anvil, torch, and hammer. While we were standing there, he created a small hook. It took a long time and much effort. I cannot imagine how

Coming soon!

FASHION FORWARD

FASHION MYTHS—BUSTED!

It's a myth that starting your own business is easy. The fashion world, too, is full of myths.

Can you mix silver with gold? Yes, all the time! Often, you'll find a piece with both silver and gold, and that makes the piece more wearable.

Can you wear white in winter? It used to be that you couldn't wear white after Labor Day. Now we do it all the time and call it winter white! You can take a pair of white jeans that you'd wear with a tank top in summer and pair it with a chunky sweater and boots in winter.

Must your bag and belt match your shoes? Absolutely not! Match your shoes to your top— not necessarily an exact match, but a top will read "brown" or "black." Match your shoes and belt accordingly.

many hours it took to make our floor-to-ceiling displays, but I know they were painstakingly made with love. They are so unique; everyone who comes in comments on them. Each one is different, like so many things at Frox. The displays house the clothing in such an artistic way, spiraling up toward the ceiling, creating a growing vine effect. The artist still comes by to visit and admire them.

"I was never in the fashion industry—until now," he jokes.

As my grand opening neared, all my insecurities came flooding in. I gained a lot of knowledge from the store owners I worked with. They all gave me advice and told me I would be fine. But this was a new aspect of the industry for me. I asked myself, *Can I do what they have done? What will the town think of this shop? What will they think of me?* I knew I had to believe in myself or how would others believe in me. I dug deep and remembered the quote that Brené Brown says began her journey— because it also began mine.

It is from Theodore Rosevelt's speech, *The Man in the Arena*

> *"It is not the critic who counts: not the man who points out how the strong man stumbles, or where the doer of deeds could have done them better. The credit belongs to the man who is actually in the arena, whose face is marred by dust and sweat and blood… who at the best knows in the end the triumph of high achievement, and who at the worst, if he fails, at least fails while daring greatly."*

I was going to dare greatly. This passage resonates with me, and anytime I need a little courage, I refer back to it.

On September 2003, I held my grand opening. My heart swelled with pride in all that I was creating. In Frox, I created a place where women feel comfortable, but also a place where *I* feel comfortable. I fit perfectly. Frox is the place where everyone belongs. I prepared for months through the construction, then carefully curating the collections of clothing, gifts, and jewelry that would be my first impression. I imagined the gals who would shop here, and I wondered, what would they like and what would they need. I observed many curious onlookers peeking through the kraft paper on the windows. I was excited to meet them and start this new journey.

I knew this was my big shot, my opportunity to help empower women like so many women who threaded through my life. I had left repping, and I had no plan B. This was it. Failure was not really an option. My husband and I invested a lot into the store, and I had to make it work. The other store owners I knew made it look easy. But as I have learned, retail is not for the faint of heart. When our customers walk in, all the displays are merchandised to perfection. Little do they know five minutes before, we were cleaning, ripping open boxes, hanging, and steaming. Just like the knit down: What it looks like at the start is not what you see after the dyebath.

When I opened Frox, Perkasie was still a small town. I knew it was imperative that I become a part of the community. People buy from people they like, know, and trust. I quickly made friends in my new town. My friends became my customers, and my customers became my friends. I was eager to belong, and so I got involved. Almost immediately, I joined an organization called Perkasie Town Improvement Association. This organization was established after the great Perkasie fire, which burned down the main part of town. The goal was to help businesses get back on their feet, and it still is the goal today after COVID. I wanted to be a part of that. I volunteered for many groups in town and made an impact on my small corner of the world. It was a lot of early meetings, helping with events, and lots of running around on the day of the event, helping in any capacity I could.

It felt good to be part of my community. As a sales rep traveling the country, I was not home enough to make strong connections. Amazingly the majority of our businesses in town are run by women. These women are fierce and driven. They have great passion, vision, and commitment to their families and communities. I am honored to be among them and to be the empowered woman that I saw so early in my youth.

Our town is off the beaten track, and my store is as well. So, I needed to attract customers to my street. I was fortunate to be on a committee that began planning events that really brought attention to Perkasie. Over the years, these events have grown, such as our holiday tree lighting that attracts thousands of people and is documented as the oldest tree lighting in the country, and our summer farmers' market, which has also taken off. To this day, we continue to find unique ways to help people find our hidden gem in Bucks County.

Creating our store windows was a tremendous pleasure. I set up the window before our grand opening to show it was a lifestyle store—more than a clothing boutique. Back then, lifestyle stores were a new concept. I needed to communicate that we sold clothes but also home décor,

Grand opening window

Making the ordinary extraordinary

jewelry, and gifts. I wanted an all-inclusive shop in merchandise and culture.

So, in preparation for the big day, I dressed mannequins holding shopping bags. I placed a Parisian vintage clock by a line called America Retold. There was a table where people could enter to win the clock—helping me to begin my customer list and making my introduction to the town.

That first holiday season, the window was a winter wonderland theme. We filled the windows with imitation snow and created an ice pond with mirrors placed on the window floor. There were skates and sleds throughout the window. I loved re-creating scenes from the pictures in my head from my many trips to NYC. We change our window

Our violinist

theme about once a month. I try to give the windows challenging, provocative themes.

Our themed window displays are designed to delight and inspire women. One month, we celebrated every-body by displaying photos of our clients holding glittering apples or pears representing their own body shape. Because Every-Body is a Frox girl.

Another month, we created an elaborate display of water bottles repurposed and cut into flowers in large pots and watering cans, turning recycling from the ordinary to extraordinary. They were spectacular windows, and they have even got the attention of the press.

Each holiday season, a local violinist plays holiday music in our window. I am so grateful to have such a talented woman grace us every year since day one. She

Living christmas trees

has commented that, "No matter how busy I am with holiday concerts and events, I always make time for Frox because it is not Christmas without playing in the window."

I designed Christmas tree skirts on mannequins out of greens, ribbons, and ornaments. It looks like they are living Christmas trees dressed to the nines. Hundreds of people come to see the windows, hear the holiday music, and light up the town tree. It harkens back to a simpler time.

From my very first time I spied my store, I knew I would speak to my gals through my windows. The windows are an outlet to express my creativity and point of

(continued on page 136)

FASHION FORWARD

Speaking of skirts, skirts and dresses are easier to buy than pants because you don't have to worry about rise—the space from your belly button down. Women are wearing skirts and dresses less, but they are still wardrobe staples. In the summer, I sell a lot of them. I sell more dresses than skirts. Here's how to choose:

- **If you are a pear, choose an A-line.** Shaped like an A, it skims over the hips.
- **If you are an apple, look for a waistline above your belly.** A straight pencil skirt will be best for you.
- **A wrap dress is a safe choice for most women.** It's universally flattering to most body shapes. In 1972, Diane von Furstenberg designed the wrap dress. It is still one of her best-selling pieces, as it is in Frox as well.
- **Choose the hem length depending on your height.** If you are petite, wear a length above your knee because it shows more leg and makes you look taller. If you're taller, you can wear a midi, which falls mid-calf. Most women can wear a maxi, which falls to your ankles. That works for everyone—though if you're shorter, you might need to hem it.
- **Skip the slip.** Nobody wears slips anymore. I don't even own one! If something is sheer enough that you could see through it, it should have a lining. If not, don't buy it!

view. When people are standing outside and pointing at our windows, it fills me with joy.

Inside Frox, I wanted to have much more than the standard department store dressing rooms: cramped closets with white walls, cold floors, horrible mirrors, and bad lighting. Often when I try something on in one of those dressing rooms, I conclude that I look better in the clothing that I already own.

Another challenge at department stores is that there's usually no one helping you try on clothes. So, if you're in the dressing room and realize you need a different color or

Buttoned Up

VALUE YOUR CLIENTS

Frox has always been about so much more than clothing. It's how we make people feel.

This advice is applicable to whatever business you are in. As Maya Angelou said, "I've learned that people will forget what you said, people will forget what you did, but people will never forget how you made them feel." Try your best to make people feel great. Put them at ease with your words and body language. Make them feel valued by listening to them and meeting their needs. I like to make them feel special by going the extra mile and providing extra value, giving them knowledge and confidence long after they leave the shop.

size, you have to get re-dressed, go back out to the floor, get the other clothing, return to the dressing room, and get undressed to try on the new clothes. It's not a pleasant shopping experience. It's too much trouble, and most women give up.

Instead, Frox dressing rooms are open and airy. They're painted a warm color with lots of hooks and areas for our girls to put down their keys, bag, and worries and get them ready for a great experience.

Outside the fitting rooms is a warm welcoming area set up as a cozy living room with large full-length mirrors, deep soft chairs, fluffy pillows, and a dig-your-toes-in rug. As the Frox girls emerge from spacious fitting rooms, which many have said are bigger than their first New York apartment, we anxiously sit on the chairs and wait to see the fashions. We offer our expertise from all of our many years in the business. We chat and tell stories. We want them to feel like they are shopping with friends—because they are. Before they know it, the transformation begins. We help them learn about what works on their unique shapes, and before their eyes, they see themselves in a different light. We all feel vulnerable when dealing with body image, but Frox is a safe place where we all are connected. We help them to love and accept themselves.

(continued on page 140)

FASHION FORWARD

What should you wear to Saturday's farmers' market, errand running, date night out? Jeans, of course. Every woman needs a good pair of jeans.

Here's how to buy yours.

- **Look for the proper fit.** Look at the rise: is it too high or too low? Across your bum and leg: Is it too high, or too loose? Consider the length: is it too short or too long?

- **Consider a fabric with some stretch and Lycra.** This helps jeans retain their shape and hold up to many washings. Wearing jeans with some stretch is also much more comfortable and is great for gals who are on the move because the jeans move with them all day.

- **Choose a clean, classic look.** If you want to address a trend like tears, holes, embroidery, or bedazzling, buy only one pair for the season, knowing it may not be in for next season.

- **For color:** Dark denim is dressier; faded or light is more casual. Medium blue is the best choice for every day.

- **If you're petite,** avoid a wide or flared leg. It'll make you look shorter.

- **If you're curvy,** a flare might balance out the hip to give a long lean look

If you want your jeans to last a long time, wash them on the gentle cycle and put them on a drying rack. Don't use heat, which breaks down the Lycra fibers, much like a dry rubber band. It's best to wash jeans only after every four or five wearings.

Standing outside that fitting room, I am grateful that they open up to me and express their vulnerability.

I listen to them, what they like and what they don't like. So, when I go to the trade shows, they are all in my head. As I walk by a booth, I think, *That is perfect for my Frox gals; they will love this.* As I select each piece in the line, I think of their body shapes and what will work for

BEAUTIFUL
INSIDE AND OUT

BE KIND TO YOURSELF

Day after day, I watch women criticize themselves at Frox. I've stood outside these dressing rooms almost every day for the past two decades, and not one woman has walked out of the dressing rooms and proclaimed, "I look amazing!"

Their eyes are drawn to their perceived figure flaws like laser beams:

I'm too fat.
I'm too thin.
My thighs are too big.
My breasts are too small.

I don't see what you see! I see you as a beautiful person. Remember, other people are not drawn to your flaws—they see the whole you. They aren't being critical of you, largely they're thinking about themselves.

them and what won't. I think of their lifestyles and what I can see them getting a lot of use out of. Then I tell a story with the clothes, knowing they will be merchandised together. I make sure they all "talk to each other." There is no digging in bins or sorting through racks. As you walk in the door, you are swept away with a visual array of colors and textures, all designed to inspire and delight as your eye

What are your best figure assets? Do you have great legs? Are your arms toned and strong? Train yourself to hone in on your strengths first. Blur over the rest.

And please, know how to take a compliment!

If I had a dollar for every time a woman dismissed a compliment, I could move to Tahiti. We are conditioned to be modest—to the point of self-deprecation. When I tell a woman, "You look amazing. That dress drapes over your body beautifully," it is very hard to get her to see it. Usually, her response is to focus on this flaw or that one.

Learn how to take a compliment. It's as easy as saying, "Thanks."

Better still if you can add, "I got it at Frox."

Frox dressing rooms

dances from display to display, each fully coordinated look conjuring up thoughts of how you will feel and where you will go in these looks.

Over the years, my clients have evolved. I even dress

FASHION FORWARD

HOLD THE LINE

For a slimming effect, make your clothing line flow from your head to your toes. Use clothing to look long and lean.

This can be done with color, wearing one color from head to toe. To avoid breaking the line, don't wear too many layers. They break the line and make you look shorter than you are.

Stand back and see the entire look from head to toe. Check to see if lines are broken. Consider adding a focal point to a part of your body you want to accentuate.

A lot of times I have my ladies put on long necklaces to lengthen the body and sometimes statement necklaces to highlight the face.

some of their grown children. We have come on the journey with them: birthdays, anniversaries, graduations, weddings. We like to think a piece of Frox is with them on all their travels. We encourage them to snap selfies in all the places they have been so they can see how beautiful they look and so can others.

Every-Body is a Frox girl

The common thread since day one is the ability to go from work to weekend to a night out with just a few pieces—not a lot of pieces, but the right ones that will last for years to come.

One of the best parts of my job continues to be going to the NYC fashion shows and trade shows. But now, I'm on the other side of the booth—a buyer, not a seller. I visit the vendors whose clothing is the right fit for my customers to learn about their lines the designer's point of view, and how the clothing is made. I'm the bridge between those vendors and my customers.

I choose each and every piece of merchandise for Frox with great care. My gals are always top of mind. I know their lives are busy. It's my job to curate the clothing that will fit their lifestyle.

From the beginning, I wanted Frox to be more than just a store—a community. Right away, I started to hold events, to entertain and inspire them. It was very early girl-friend marketing. We held so many fun events. We would let our imaginations fly. Our purpose was to always have girls feel special and pampered. One memorable event was our Pedi & Bubble Night. We thought, *how can we give them a spa experience, but still allow them to shop? We can't do facials because they're too messy, nor manicures and possibly having wet polish on our clothing, but they could have it on their toes.* So Pedi & Bubbles was born. A local spa brought in tubs and placed them around the store. The ladies had

Frox signature packaging

their toes done, grabbed some bubbly, and shopped in their flip-flops. It was a sight. We have had a casino night where they played games to win Frox dollars, PJ parties with all the staff and customers in jammies and pigtails, fun finger-food, wine tastings, jewelry making, and so many more. Frox became the gathering place I dreamed of.

I want our guests to feel that shopping at Frox is like receiving a special gift.

Every package is wrapped with our leopard signature paper or placed in fashionable bags with seasonal, unique tissue paper with a carefully placed bow.

It is so important to cater to special segments of my customer base. Young moms, for example, have a hard time getting away to shop. For them, I hold lunchtime special events when the kids go back to school called "Kids Away; It's Time to Play." We also do our "Lunch Time Live," which is a Facebook Live video filled with tips and shopping that they can watch from their homes or their desks.

I appreciate the challenges of being a mother with young children. When I was a young mom myself, sometimes my two children came to Frox. My son would wear headphones and watch the TV in the play area we had set up for kids. He would be giggling about something he was watching, which amused my customers. "We don't know what he's laughing about, but he brings joy to the store," they would tell me. My daughter helped behind the counter, and she got to see me engage with women and empower them through fashion. She saw that it was wonderful when women helped other women. Now she is in the fashion industry and is making her own mark on the world. And my son, much like me, is inspired to help people and make a difference in their lives. They both have had their own dyebaths to endure. These are their stories to tell. But as a parent, all I can do is love them unconditionally and know that when they emerge from each dyebath, they will be unique and continue to transform, always re-creating another fabric for that time in their lives.

Frox has always been about family, community, and

our desire to give back. As a result, over the years, we have held many private shopping parties, sometimes just to raise money for local charities. We are known to close the store just to cater to a group, donating a percentage of the proceeds to their designated charity. I now have the ability to give back to my community. The policy in our store is that whenever anyone comes in asking for a donation to support a cause, the answer is always, "YES." Like Audrey Hepburn said: As you grow older, you will discover that you have two hands—one for helping yourself, the other for helping others.

I work hard to connect my Perkasie community with my NYC community. When I return from the New York shows, my Perkasie customers eagerly ask, "What did you see?" An "aha" moment came when I realized we should show them by re-creating the NYC experience. So, I held our first fashion show, complete with red carpet, fast music, swag bags, and chair cards with each customer's name and seat number on them. Our fashion shows make them feel so special. I use customers as models. They are realistic sizes—from 4 to 14, all ages from 18 to 85. All their unique bodies look beautiful. At the end, all the customer-models line up on stage. It is a powerful moment—a real celebration of women.

As I remember our first fashion show, I realize how far

Frox fashion show

we have come. At first, we thought we would have it in the store, clear it out, and put chairs down the middle. But within the first week, we sold out of tickets. We needed a bigger space. At the time, there were no event spaces in Perkasie, so we racked are brains to think of where to hold it. Then we remembered that the very place I took my daughter to gymnastics, up those steep steps so long ago, was vacant. I talked to my landlord and asked if we could use the space. He replied, "No problem, but it is dirty, and I use it as storage."

We had no choice, so we marketed it as a "loft" space above Frox, dirty and grungy as was all the rage in New

York then. We ordered a long red carpet and red rope from the internet and put six shop lights down the sides to make a makeshift runway. We used photographers paper to create a backdrop and rented 100 white chairs. The rest is history. Our customers still say this was the best fashion show. Now we hold them twice a year with many more guests and in beautiful venues. But I agree with them: This one was the best.

All of these wonderful experiences did not happen overnight, and they were not without their challenges. As Tony Robbins says, "It takes a long time to be an overnight success."

Many unexpected things happened to knock us off our feet. But each time we weighed our fabric. Weighing the fabric helps to predict if it can survive a dyebath. But sometimes in life, the outcome is unpredictable.

Over the years, we had to adapt to what was going on outside our doors. Our store opened shortly after 9/11 then Hurricane Sandy took our power out for weeks. People couldn't shop in the dark. Resolved not to close, we held candlelight shopping. In our time in business, we have had two recessions, the housing crash, construction, and parking issues, online shopping competition, and new malls being built—but no matter what came our way, we came out better and stronger—just like our clothing coming out of a dyebath.

All the challenges make the successes sweeter. I am proud of the brand I have built, although it could not have been done without the help and support of many others. I am most honored to have met and shared stories with thousands of women who threaded through my life.

Just when I thought I had seen it all, along came COVID-19. As I write this book, we are living through a global pandemic. This has changed all of us, and it changed Frox, too. COVID has been so challenging because so much of it is outside of my control. The governor saying, "You must shut down," was devastating. Never before in any challenge were we forced to close our doors.

I watched many local business owners crawl into a hole. Many closed their doors—some for good. I refused to do that. I continued to do the only thing I know how to do, what I've been doing for years: stick to my WHY. I know sometimes our setbacks are actually setups.

Our town stood up to this new challenge and supported each other. Clients have been coming to Frox whom I haven't seen in many years to connect, craving community, and supporting small businesses because if they don't, many will not be there in the future.

I believe you can learn and grow—even thrive—from just about any challenge. COVID is no exception. A big, red pause button was pushed on the world. So many families were spiraling: two working parents running around with over-scheduled kids, far too many of them suffering from anxiety. I believe collectively we all began to appreciate the smallest things. So many have been thrown into their own dyebaths, facing challenges with businesses, loneliness, depression, and loss of family members. But in any situation, there is a silver lining.

Before COVID, when were you grateful simply to go outside and breathe air? Walk around the block? Stay safe at home with your family? Lovingly prepare a home-cooked meal and eat with your family around the table? What do we have left at this point but our family and our relationships?

Right away, I doubled down on our Facebook Live event Frox in a Box. Every Tuesday night, I open my newest shipment of clothes and reveal it live.

I wanted to give customers a chance to see each other, connect, and continue some normalcy. I began the first Live event by saying, "I'm not going to talk about COVID. I'm not going to talk about masks. You get enough of that on the TV."

Instead, we forgot about the outside world for an hour. We looked at pretty clothes, and we had a party online—much like the parties we have in non-pandemic times in

COVID fashion show

person at Frox, but now from their cozy couches. Those events provided a way for our girls to connect with me virtually when they couldn't connect with me personally. We were able to keep our doors open and donate as best as we could, sometimes not with money but our time in helping others. Reflecting back after a year of this world crisis, I see that we are forever changed for better or worse. For me, it gave me the gift of time. Time that I had to be with my children, to write this book, and to categorize my life and focus on what's important. Much like the first step in the dyebath, you must categorize the fabric into its origin so you know how to treat it.

There is more of a sense of comradery knowing that we have all been in this dyebath together. Women show up for women, and during this crisis so many women showed up for me and I for them. As the African proverb says: If you want to go far, go together.

CHAPTER 8

Buttoning Things Up

OVER THE MANY YEARS, FROX HAS GROWN from a little store in Perkasie to a powerhouse that has influenced thousands of women.

It isn't about money. It never has been. I believe that if you stick to your core beliefs, and your motivation to help and serve others, the money will come. My success comes from making people happy. That's what fulfills me. Success for me is about helping, connecting, and empowering women. That is my WHY.

We all face dyebaths of our own. I have had my share in both my personal life and my business life. I believe that a lot of the things I endured were not random—just like clothing is not just thrown into the dyebath. There is intent: just the right amount of dye and water, the appropriate amount of heat, and the correct number of paddles to distribute the dye to make the fabric strong and beautiful. I had to endure dark days: the heat, pressure, and challenges from family, work, and home. But these dyebaths were essential to make me who I am today. When these things happen to you, you can choose to weave them into your life, or you can leave them as salvage of fabric left on the cutting-room floor. I know that I emerged from my dyebath with more texture, color, depth, and strength than when I entered. Many of my challenges I did not choose, but they changed me forever.

I know that we will all continue to weave our fabrics together as a society and a world. We will all emerge better, stronger, and able to take on challenges because we have been through the dyebath of life.

This book is the bridge to my dream life, sharing my message, empowering and inspiring as many people as possible. With tenacity and resilience, you can reach your goals.

These are the stories that thread us together...

Share Your Story

WE ARE ALL INTERWOVEN; stories weave us together. I've shared my stories. Now it's your turn to share your story! I'd love to consider including it in my upcoming book series: *Stories that Thread Us Together: What Happens Behind the Button.*

Visit my website jillstricklandbrown.com and fill out the form to share your story.

Questions for Book Clubs

WHAT WAS YOUR FAVORITE part of the book?

Did you re-read any passages? If so, which ones?

Did the reading impact your mood? If so, how?

What surprised you most about the book?

How did your opinion of the book change as you read it?

If you could ask the author anything, what would it be?

How does the book's title work in relation to it's contents?

If you could give the book a new title, what would it be?

Did this book remind you of any other books?

How did it impact you?

Do you think you'll remember it in a few months or years?

Who do you most want to read this book?

Are there lingering questions from the book you're still thinking about?

ACKNOWLEDGMENTS

I HAVE HAD SO MANY MENTORS and teachers in my life.

First, I would like to acknowledge my family:

My children, who I learn from every day. I am so proud of the amazing people they have become.

My husband, who has supported me for many years.

My sister Tracy, who helped me through this entire process, my guiding light, and rock.

My mother, who showed me what it was like to be an empowered woman.

My brother and sisters, who have influenced me throughout my life.

My friends—too many to name, but you know who

you are—for going on this crazy journey with me and supporting me even when I wanted to give up.

My publisher Jennifer, who took my daily calls and helped me find my voice.

My publicist Rita, who invited me into the writing world.

My beloved Frox girls, who gave me the love and wisdom that is woven through this book.

To all the strong women threaded through my life who make up the fabric that is me.

And, of course, to the One who gives us all. There are many moments in writing this book that I knew He was guiding me to my life's purpose.

I know He has a plan for me greater than I can imagine, and I cannot wait to go live it.

ABOUT THE AUTHOR

JILL STRICKLAND BROWN is an entrepreneur, author, and founder of Frox, making her way in the fashion industry for more than 30 years, including working as a seven-figure sales rep and owning successful luxury boutiques. She organizes events to connect with and empower women.

Jill is a champion of her community, striving to inspire women and fellow entrepreneurs. She serves on several community organizations and boards. She is a featured contributor in the book *Success Reimagined: Inspiring Stories of Local Leaders.*

Jill is a free-spirited, out-of-the-box, and everything-is-possible kind of girl. She shares her "can do" message of inspiration and empowerment through her contagious charisma with everyone she encounters.

She resides in Pennsylvania, enjoys spending time with her family, and invites the next chapter of life with open arms in a running-baste-stitch kind of mindset.